THIS IS DIRT

A collection of writings
to inspire thought and action.

AMBER J. JENSEN

HANK

FROM THE AUTHOR

This book is based on the life and experiences of me, Amber -- a wife, mother, daughter, sister, granddaughter, writer, artist, and numerous other unfinished titles and hobbies. The experiences shared in these writings are my own and my hope is to touch, move and inspire the humans that read my words. The eclectic nature of this compilation allows for readers to open to any page and read for enjoyment, to feel not alone or just to connect.

Although this book pulls pieces of my life from a 7 year span, it has not been compiled chronologically. My brain is often scattered and my thoughts are rarely linear, so, I removed that strategy from the space of my book. I'm not a big fan of constraint.

If you find yourself nodding, crying, or even looking up and wishing you could just make eye contact with someone, please reach out to someone.

I'm here, I'm real and so are you. I see you.

XO,
Amber

ACKNOWLEDGEMENTS

I'm grateful to every person that has ever intentionally moved their eyes over the words I've smashed together.

I'm thankful for my husband and mudbugs, without whom, I'd likely not be alive and would never have anything of interest to share... or I would, it just wouldn't be nearly as entertaining.

To the coaches, CJ and GJB - I'm not certain either of you fully grasp your impact on the world and, of course, me. Seriously though, you've both coached me at quite different turns in my life -- both of you have caused transformation beyond your reckoning.

To the team at RM, I learned more working with you in the last year than I ever could have in years of buying books and navigating a campus. The way I use words will never be the same.

To my various English teachers, Mrs. H, Mr. F, and Mrs. L -- You always pushed me to use my words. Thank you for believing in me and seeing what I didn't.

It may seem odd to add this next one, and it's getting awfully long, so, here goes...

YOU!!!

Thank you, the person holding this book in your hands right this moment. Thank you for following my journey, taking a chance on a recommendation of a friend or thinking this may be an ok read because of the awesome cover. Thank you for supporting me and my work.

DEDICATION

For the man that holds me up when no one else sees me break. The man that knew I'd write a book even when I stopped believing. The man that knows how my brain works and still comes home from work to be with me.

Thank you. I choose you.

For Scott, you know how much I love your beard, yet you shave it off. I know how much you love my fiction, yet I started with non-fiction. Let's call it even.

♥ Amber

CONTENTS

PART 1: WHAT THE HECK WAS I THINKING?!

PART 2: MOMSISTENTIALISM

PART 3: SECRETS ARE MEANT TO BE TOLD

PART 4: NO ONE TALKS ABOUT THIS STUFF

PART 5: ODES AND NOTES

PART 6: COMPLETELY INCOMPLETE

PART **1**

WHAT THE HECK WAS I THINKING?!

"Because, I only have one stinking life to leave a legacy - to empower others, to make a difference - make an impact and leave my incompleteness, completely, for the world, for my kids and for myself."

WHAT THE HECK WAS I THINKING?!

Let's get this out of the way, straight out of the gate.

What was I thinking, compiling a bunch of words I've written, words I've hidden, words I've shared or not shared? What the heck was I thinking when I thought that I could smash them all together, shuffle them about and then write pretty prose to tie it all together?

What was I thinking when I thought,
"Hey, you know what, I'm always quitting, what if I finish something -- what if I finish it all at once and what if it's awesome?"

The truth, the bold, just fell out of my mouth -- truth.

I wasn't.

I finally wasn't thinking. I finally stopped overthinking it and decided to choose. I decided that if I finally just put something together, and put my most authentic self into pulling a thread of commonality through it all, I might -- just maybe -- complete something worthwhile.

When I went about the task of searching for books that would ultimately hug this book on a shelf, or come up in searches alongside it, I realized, there's a box that books fit in. There's even a box that books that don't fit in that box fit into.

This book didn't really fit in any of them. It's not a memoir, it's not a self-help book and it's not fiction.

I'm not saying this is some newfangled awesomeness -- I'm saying that I'm not sure where it fits and I'm done figuring it out.
Because, life.
Because, time.

Because, I only have one stinking life to leave a legacy, to empower others, to make a difference, make an impact and leave my incompleteness, completely, for the world, for my kids and for myself.

Maybe it's a book on momming. Maybe it's a book on existing and keeping the tendrils of yourself alive while learning to thrive in a new chapter of life. Maybe it's really about you. Or, it could be all about me and I'm just being delusional in thinking that it will connect. I don't think that's the case, but I'm willing to admit that it could be seen that way. And also, that I have reached a state of not caring. And that state of being holds incredible freedom.

Freedom to be. Freedom to create. Freedom to share.

HOLDING IT IN...

I've held myself in for years. Knowing that I've had something to say, something to contribute and the words that would carry the message, barring that inside for several years has nearly torn me apart.

Often times, when I sit down to write, I just gaze at the screen, wondering, wishing the words would come. They do, but I wall them in and force them down because they're not good enough, it's too hard and the struggle seems to be more of an addiction than the calling. Or, I puke them out, in some blog post or social media shares. They get lost in the scroll of life and limited attention span.

I've written enough words over the past few years to fill many books. Facebook posts, little rants and blog posts here and there. Yet, I pulled away and struggled with actually writing my book. And here's the thing, the deep tugging that I'm present to is nearly unrecognizable as fear...

I live and breathe like I have no fear. I don't feel it creep over me at night and I don't hold it in my gut when I walk to a mic to share my story. Yet, I wonder. I wonder if it morphed into something more sinister.

A glimpse of it shows up when I set myself in motion. I can smell it leaching from my skin after I've gutted and tidied my home office. I can feel it swimming in my stomach when I drink my second cup of coffee while I busy myself with anything but writing. I can hear it whisper in my ear as I lie in bed, just before sleep pulls me under, it's voice hissing against my thoughts.

Fear has somehow shifted into a bold confidence that needs no action. I know that I am capable of doing everything I say, and so the curled coward leans forward and croaks, "don't."

It's a bit more like arrogant complacent resignation.

I got present to this today as I stared down at a seemingly endless list of things I have promised myself that I would accomplish. Books to write and publish, paintings to create and hang, contributions to make. All of it sitting on paper or in my mind, held hostage by the idea that I don't need to do any of it because I've got nothing to prove.

That voice, it tells me that no one knows me. It whispers that I'm better off not putting it out there, not contributing to a world so choked with information that we all lack the wisdom to just be still. The voice prods me, inspires me, gives me so many ideas that I might never accomplish them all...so why even try.

A wise man recently told me that my struggle was my book. Not that I struggle to write my book but that my actual process of struggle was what I needed to share with the world. I sat with that for weeks and then I really got something from his contribution.

I have spent my life in a cycle and as I've transformed my way of being and increased my level of communication and interaction with the ontology of life, I've increased my struggle.

At one point my struggle was with holding the secret of having been sexually molested, assaulted and physically abused as a child. I carried that secret with me for over 26 years. It was the secret that gave me the feeling of power over others. The reality was that no power existed inside the story I had built about all of it.

With my struggle I was special. I was different. No one really knew me and if they thought they did that just proved to me that they really didn't and couldn't possibly be connected to me. In the darkest days of that struggle, the secret was my life ring. Opportunities to share the secret came and went and with each passing opportunity I got to dig myself in that much deeper. Then I could have guilt, like the frosting on the big cake. I'd carefully groom the edges, smooth it all out so no one would suspect.

Every time I didn't share was another stone in my path of struggle. One more emotional tripping hazard to tend to. The struggle made it all so important. So significant.

Eventually, there was an opportunity to break free of what had always been and when I took that leap, my entire life and experience of myself shifted. It was like my life had been nothing but an experience of myself in a struggle. A fight, an endless fight against what I knew I should do and what I kept not doing. The struggle had become less about keeping the abuse a secret and more about guarding that I had kept it a secret. I had been so consumed by avoidance and protecting my little struggle story that I didn't know I wasn't living.

I stood at a mic and told a room full of people about my story. I stood there and even as the words left my mouth, my voice knew that things would never ever be the same again. The biggest struggle of my life had been spoken and in speaking it into existence I realized just how much of my life had been suffocated by it. Every aspect, every breath, the whole web of my existence was tangled by this struggle.

When I sat down, I was shaken. The agitation I felt was deep and churning. The voice was overridden. It hadn't won and for the first time in probably ever, I had taken the lead. When I left that room I swear I had never smelled air so crisp or felt a breeze so sweet.

The actions of my life since that one big coup d'etat against my inner voice have been scattered. I've learned that no one is going to write my story for me and that there is someone out there in the world that needs to hear it. If I hold this discovery and make this a new struggle, they will struggle and I will struggle and then we will both die and our lives will be a series of social media accounts left dormant and love notes left unsent. The sharing brings it to life. The actual physicality of bringing it into the open and letting it breathe. That's where the shift occurs. That's where the contribution is made.

START, STALL, START OVER

I wouldn't say I'm a quitter. I'd describe myself as more of a non-finisher. I tend to take on projects that sound fun, interesting and present a challenge. Then, as the initial challenge of startup morphs into something closer to commitment, I feel my feet get tingly and then a touch cool. For the next week or so, I encounter innumerable reasons and circumstances that prohibit the furthering of said project. My feet then make the full transformation from cool and clammy to rock solid glacial blocks. Shame, embarrassment, lack of integrity... Those are the seeds that take root when I abandon a project.

Here's the way it plays out...

I announce to the world that I am going to accomplish X, I then move, take action and discover that I may not know all the pieces I need for the puzzle to be complete, then Y happens and then I feel Z and act on those feelings.

It's the same victimmy equation every time. As I sit here — desperately willing my thumbs to work on this new sized iPhone — I'm tempted to use this cumbersome technology as another excuse. I don't know why I do what I do. I don't know why I leave half finished things lying around like bread crumbs on my life path. I just do.

Now, just because I did, doesn't mean I should continue on that way. Recognizing and admitting there is a problem is the first step to change and there is only change in relation to the past. Full and total transformation would be a better goal. Oh, yeah, I'm going there. This isn't about writing or not writing a blog, a book or a piece of copy for a client. This is about keeping my word. It's about being the person I know I am and not allowing circumstances to rule my world. The only truth is when I take action on my word.

Now, several pages down, the rest of my life to go. There have been many direction changes since I first began this journey. This should be an interesting ride.

THE STRUGGLE IS REAL

I've grappled with sharing what I'm up to for quite a while. When we don't share what we're dreaming, wanting and actively pursuing it does something insidious.

It protects us.

It also eats us alive.

It protects us from being seen as a failure, a risk-taker, a dreamer and even a liar. It protects us from shame, humiliation and loss. At the same time it holds us in its cold embrace — it stifles us and convinces us that solitary dreaming is the only safety. It causes us to question our worth and even our sanity at times. This secret safety removes responsibility and accountability.

This is a double edged sword.

If no one knows the deepest desire in our hearts — our burning passion — then there's no one there to laugh at our failure, cheer us on, point out our flaws, offer us guidance and coaching, kick us when we're down or offer a hand when we stumble.

These words should be written and published on a blog, or a book. My blog. My book. These words should be touching someone's life - just waiting to read this to not feel alone. These words don't belong on Facebook as a status update. It is meant to be written somewhere I've been avoiding. I've been stifling my own dreams. Waiting for 'someday.'

What am I up to? I'm hiding. I'm saving draft after draft. I've been hiding for a long time. I've been hiding something special. Me. I'm awesome. I'm vibrant. I have things to say and people to help. I have no idea what the next step is for me and that locks me up. I am terrified of vulnerability and failure and if I step out into the unknown... All I know is I'm on fire. I'm burning up. I have got to channel this passion into creating something beautiful. I have the ability to draw out the greatness in others and show it to them in a way they never thought possible for themselves. I have a gift. I'm blessed. My gift is to shine light on all the dreams, passions and flickering flames that lie hiding behind excuses, reasons and stories.

You are fabulous and whether you know it or not, you have a gift too. My blessing is helping to uncover that gift, that dream, that passion and fan that timid flame until it burns so hot that you can't stand to sit there hiding it.

My dream, my passion is this... I'll speak as if it's reality because our words create our reality. I am an author, a coach, a nurturer, a sage. There is no one in the world like me and no one with my unique insight into the deeper workings of digging out the greatness in others.

PART **2**

MOMSISTENTIALISMS

"We do the best we
can -- and then, we
do even better -- but
sometimes we don't,
and for those times,
it helps to know we're
not alone."

MOMTOLOGY.
MOMSISTENTIALISM.
PHEMOMENOLOGY.

Life. Momming. Parenting. Adulting. Chaos.

I've recently been using the term momtology to describe my momming style. Momtology. Momsistentialism. Phemomenogy.

For any of you that need to know what you're about to get into, here's the jist of it.

I've been avoiding writing a book for years. I avoided it by writing down thoughts and insights that I wished to share but became a distraction from the bigger project. That avoidance became this book.

You'll get a bit of existentialist phenomenological ontology in the space of parenting, mothering, relationships, personal development, pregnancy, loss, work, not working, loneliness, and other adulting topics. If you have experience with ontological education like Landmark Education -- or are familiar with the works of Martin Heidegger, Gary John Bishop, Werner Erhard, Gustav Bergmann... anyway, you get the idea, these are the thinkers that inspire me. I consume their content and smear it around my life. There's an undercurrent of distinct language that may seem off from the usual and there's an intentional way of being about that.

Am I a modern philosopher? I don't know, maybe, maybe not. I do like to think, figure myself out, grow where I can and share with others so they can get what they're going to get from me and be who they're going to be with all of that.

So, if you're still with me...
Let's do it anyway.

It's said that compassion changes everything.
I think word changes everything.

How we linguistically frame our lives, situations and selves creates the existence we live in. When we share stories or dreams, the way we speak in human interactions, it all moves the space and creates the tone.

When I discovered ontology, I discovered that I create my own life. Not in the Rumi quote sort of way, but in the complete and utterly unfathomable miraculousness of speaking what will be so.

I've collected my writings from the past few years. All the avoidance pieces that had me focus away from a goal.

There are letters to my children, personal journal entries, poems, essays, contest writings never entered, social media posts expanded on and blog posts.

The act of completing all of this incomplete work, all of these words I wrote to avoid the words I really wanted to say, it pulls itself together in a kaleidoscope view into what it is to be human and fight against the deepest desires of a soul.

In threading these seemingly lone beads onto a common string, and adding accents to pull it all together, I believe I will contribute strength to those that become resigned to their own self imposed reasons and circumstance.

If I can leave you with just one thing, if you've already decided to close this book and move along — I say, to you, of your dream, that goal you can't shake, that image that pesters you in the wee hours...

Do it anyway.

DANCE, I WON'T STOP YOU

Yesterday was my oldest's last day of preschool. There was a potluck to celebrate. The room was packed. Two classes of preschoolers, their parents, siblings and a few grandparents. First the participation awards were given. Then the eating and after that, a slideshow of photos from the school year.

As I sat there, holding my youngest, watching photos of kids in the other class I noticed the little kids up at the front of the room. Instantly, I spotted my son.

He danced.

He stood in a group of his peers and danced. He was the only one. The others looked to him and back at their parents or down at their coloring books. Still, he danced.

He danced the way only he can. It's like a combination of a ballet dancer, a monkey and a raver. Soon, a little girl joined him. They danced like they were the only two that could hear the music.

They laughed.

The rest of us sat, studious, in our chairs watching a boring as hell slideshow of kids we didn't really know. Then, one by one, the little kids joined the dancing. My heart filled and my eyes welled over.

By the time the teacher made her way to the front of the dim room and crouched down to settle the dancers many children were dancing in laps and around the legs of the adults. It never once occurred to me to make my son stop dancing. It never occurred to me that he shouldn't just jump up and dance when his heart felt the music.

My heart crushed for each of the children that were subdued. I watched as parents crept between chairs to follow what the teacher did. Quiet those precious souls.

I understand why the teacher softly quieted the dancing sprites. I get that there is a social decorum and that the slideshow was important.

But, no.

No.

NO!

The moment was then. A magical thing, all these little kids just living and laughing and being. The photos were the past. It gave me such pause that my breath hitched and stuck in my throat.

My son still danced. Quietly and to his own rhythm. He danced. He moved away from the group and danced alone.

The music cracked and distorted as it blared out of the laptop and not one other person looked upset by the stifling of the moment. Everyone sat, awkwardly holding wiggling babies and toddlers, with bored vacant expressions on their faces.

I wanted to scream. I wanted to stand on a folding table and yell at the top of my lungs.

'THIS IS NOW!'

The moment passed and more kids and parents shuffled as the blanket of restlessness settled and smothered. The next class slideshow came on and my husband retrieved our son to watch it. He wiggled and shifted on my husbands lap. Finally he got down to play with the other kids whose parents had given up tether.

The slideshow, to me, was a stark reminder of how much we hold onto what isn't even happening. We place so much importance on what was that we stifle and stuff down the joy and spontaneity of what is.

My son was in nearly every photo of his class slideshow. He didn't care. He just wanted to dance.

How many of us feel restless as we stand in the checkout line or wait in traffic? How many times do we stop ourselves from humming a song in an elevator or at a doctors office? We think of what happened that day, that week, that year. We contemplate tomorrow or next year. Our jam comes on the radio, across the crackly grocery store sound system or is playing far off in the distance. Our heart perks up for a moment and we focus on the slideshow of our life. Instead the song is over and our being gets just a bit more dehydrated. Our joy cracks.

Just dance.

Dancing can be swaying, humming, bouncing or bobbing. Dancing can be just being present to the moment. Just knowing and seeing and feeling that suppression and not resisting. Understanding that the feeling of restlessness stems from a deeper place. That can be the dance.

This morning, as I placed my sons breakfast in front of him, he moved his arms and swayed to a bluegrass song.

'Mom, I always want to dance. I just have to.'

I never ever want to stifle that. Ever.

PERSPECTIVE IS EVERYTHING

In a world where we know everything or have the answers in our pockets at all times it is quite easy to assume we are always right. The trouble with right is that there is no true pure right. It is all in perception and perspective. Reality is different for each observer.

There are so many opportunities to flex our right muscles and put others in their place. There are social media outlets, forums, comment sections and anonymity with our profile pic plastered on the front to make us feel real and open.

We share our best and hide our worst because it might not be right. We point out the flaws of others lifestyles, parenting, birthing, schooling, careers and personal choices because they aren't right.

Perhaps if we all just take a step back and not look so closely, we will find that perspective holds the key to our happiness and the wellbeing of our souls.

Life isn't meant to be dissected. It's not linear and it doesn't follow the rules for right and wrong that are so limiting and imposing these days. There is no right way to dance or sing anymore than there are right ways to parent and live.

I was coloring with my boys today and noticed the carousel horse actually looked like it had a candy striped horse wang. I noticed this because the box of crayons was sitting on top of the rest of the picture. Because I could only see what I could see, my judgment of the image was quite skewed. Yes, I knew that Crayola wouldn't illustrate a horse dong to be colored by preschoolers but just that it appeared that way for a second made me think.

It was obviously a misconception. I wasn't seeing the whole picture. How many times had that happened before with something bigger in my life. How many times had I jumped to my right idea of what should or shouldn't be because I could only see a part of the reality?

Step back. Take it all in. It's worth it. It's freeing.

MOM WINS

I'm tired of hearing about how hard it is to be a Stay-at-home-mom. I'm guilty. I've complained. I've cried in my room temperature hours old coffee. I've griped and moaned and groaned.

Enough.

We've all got our cross to bear and being a mother, any kind of mother, isn't one. It's a blessing. Children are a blessing. If you don't believe me, ask a friend or family member that suffers from infertility (10% of women in the United States suffer infertility and that's not counting any difficulties that stem from their partner). Or, better yet, complain to them about your sleepless nights and toddler tantrums. Wait to be throat punched.

Here's the deal. We all make choices as mothers. Some choose to stay home and sacrifice the wage earned in order to be at home with their brood. Others choose to work and juggle mothering with the stresses of a career. There are the outliers, the single moms that must work, the couples that barely make ends meet with two incomes and the sprinkling of other situations that didn't actively make a choice.

The thing is, it's still a choice. Even if you didn't make a direct choice to stay at home or work, at some point there was a choice made that would affect the future ability to choose staying at home or going to work.

I honestly think SAHMs complain because it's a lonely thankless task that is also freaking awesome and rather enjoyable. There's a bit of guilt to that. Guilt that leads us to complain rather than revel in the blessing that is being a mom full time at home.

Much like my choice to birth naturally, I keep being a SAHM on the DL. But why? Why not be excited and eager to share what I do? People have strong opinions and love to share them. Women have been staying home with their babies for centuries and yet I still hear this quite often, "But what do you do all day?" Or its cousin, "What else do you do?" To which I'd like to reply, "Are you effing kidding me?! Nobody died today; it was a good day."

In all seriousness, I can understand this coming from people without kids but even mothers or seasoned grandmothers ask these asinine questions. I'm pretty socially adept so I don't reply, "Bitch, you know, you know how busy it is. Why are you calling me out?!"

Can we just take a moment to breathe in, breathe out and get present to what it means to be able to stay home with the little people we raise to be productive members of society?

1. Naps. They're a serious luxury. I'd wager they're worth more than currency to some. I'd gladly take pay in naps. As a SAHM I get to take

naps. Not every day. Not always when I want to, but, I get to nap. That alone is a serious perk.

2. Say. I have say in what goes with my kids. Moms that work have say too. But, they don't have complete say. There is a lot of trust there and agreements with Daycares and Preschools. I alone have the say in what happens or doesn't happen. That's big for me.

3. Attire. I'm not going to get all cliche about my mom garb because, honestly, I don't live in ratty yoga pants. However, I wear what I want. In winter I can dress like a hobo in 15 layers of weirdness with fleece leggings and Kirkland knockoff Uggs as the staples. In summer, I can wear my bikini. I can get dressed whenever in whatever I please and no one says anything sideways about it. No more heels and stockings and slacks. No more scrubs and sneakers and worrying about schlepping home any number of odd germs. Nope. I wear what I want. Perk.

4. Food. I'm not gonna lie, it's awesome having the ability to eat what I want basically when I want. I don't have to eat out or pack a lunch or wait for a set time to cram food in my gob. I just have to make time to feed myself and usually three other little mouths.

5. Freedom. I may be tethered to these little people all day (and night) but, hey, they're mobile. I can run an errand, go to doctors appointments, shop, go on walks, go to the park, go to storytime at the library and a bunch of other super cool things while the rest of the world is working at a set place doing a set thing. It felt confining at first and I'll admit that I'm only just discovering the freedom but, it's amazing and I'm thankful for it.

6. Playing house. I get to, hypothetically, make my house a home. Now, I'm struggling with parts of that ideal but for the most part, I've got a groove down. I get to spend more time than the working mom meal planning, gardening, crafting, writing, reading, learning, cooking, cleaning, organizing and all the domestic stuff. I don't do a lot of that as

I haven't quite fit it all into the groove but I can if I want to and that's freedom.

7. That mom. I get to be that mom. The one that's always available when sick kids call from school. The mom that other moms call when they need a sitter or daycare or for emergencies. I get to offer my time to causes and volunteer and be a member of the community in a way that I couldn't if I worked outside the home. Perk. Perk. Perk.

I'm sure there are tons more but as I lie here tapping away on my phone I realize I'd like to exercise perk number one. And I can. And it's awesome. And I can say that without diminishing what I do. I'm important. I'm contributing to society just as much as working moms. And, I take naps.

I'M WEIRD AND THAT'S OK

There are a lot of opinions as to what a normal mom or normal wife and - let's be honest - a normal person - should be. I have read so much on the subject of what I should be, that I've decided, I'm not that. I won't ever be and that's totally fine. I own my weird and I hope others can too. There's a freedom in liking the off parts of oneself. There's joy in dancing your own unique dance and knowing that it is just that, your own.

Let's rip the bandage off and expose this for what it is...

1. There are more than 5 animal skulls in my freezer. I'm not even sure where they came from. I think there's a badger, a couple of coyotes, a porcupine... I forget they are there every once in awhile and get a nice surprise when I open the sacks.

2. There's a worm farm under my kitchen sink. On purpose. My husband got a wild hair to save a few red wigglers after fishing. The next day I found him and the kids shredding newspapers and soaking it with water. Now I have worms making dirt in my house. I think it's cool. I talk to them when I give them coffee grounds.

3. I often garden in my underwear. Bikinis are awesome but I don't always have time to find one. Plus, the kids and I often spend whole days in our undies. It saves on laundry. Very green.

4. I get a lot of enjoyment out of poking dead things with sticks. I poke poop too just to see what an animal ate. I touch eyeballs and hold elk guts while a hunter is trying a new animal dressing technique. I pick hair off of a hanging carcass of meat and I allow my husband to boil whole deer heads in my canner in the kitchen. Dead animals are interesting and a great opportunity to really see how life works. I dig it.

5. I employ my dogs as the first step in dishwashing. I even call one dog 'The Closer' because no one can clean a cast iron skillet like she can.

6. I'm not exactly a tidy housewife. I consider my duties as a stay-at-home person to be more along the lines of adventures with the kids, facilitating learning and making sure no one dies. The house will always be here and it'll always need some form of cleaning. I boast about my clean house when my toilets or floors are clean (not usually at the same time) and simultaneously there is crusted food on the walls. I choose my battles.

7. I think it's totally fine to pee in the shower and even encourage the kids to do it (while they're showering) to save on diapers and little boy toilet aim issues. The water all goes to the same septic system. No big deal.

So, there you have it. I like to think that normal is more of a spectrum. That way I can slide around a bit.

IT IS WHATEVER COLOR YOU SAY IT IS

While watching my oldest boy color and eat a snack simultaneously, I noticed he kept making a throaty whiney noise. I asked what the noise was that he was making.

"I'm sad for this flower. It wants to be blue but it has to be red. They're always red but all I have is blue right now."

I had to breathe and just be with that. Really get present to it. He felt something in his heart for an inanimate object that exists in color only as whatever the artist chooses. The color was his choice and yet he still felt compelled to go with the masses. How on earth he knew that tulips are usually portrayed as red, I don't know. But he felt sad about knowing it 'should' be red but he was coloring it blue.

Why?

Why is there even a 'should' for how to use an imagination? Should. That word sits heavy in the air each time I hear or use it. It implies there is something wrong here and that the right thing is a bit out of reach.

What if there was no should?

What if it was completely obliterated? Removed from the context of our lives.

I googled 'Blue Tulip'. And then turned my phone around to show him.

What I saw in his eyes nearly brought me to weeping and twisted my gut all at once. Pure and utter joy. He was relieved. He was surprised. He was ok. Blue. Blue was just as ok as red. The should had been removed.

"Mom, there are blue tulips?! Just like when I was in preschool and they said that red wasn't a boy color and I said it was my favorite anyway. Red can still be my color and the tulip can be blue and be happy."

Ouch.

Precious boy. Yes. So much yes.

Yes, he can love the color red. He can color a tulip blue. He can paint the night sky with imagined creatures or close his eyes and dream of being a dancer, a strong ballet dancer. He can color any color and be anything, because he says so. Because I say so. Because it is just that way. The way we build our world. The words we choose. The norms we believe.

He put his little head down in concentration and moved his crayon back up to the abandoned tulip. Blue. He fervently colored that beautiful flower blue. Just because. And it was perfect.

THE CAKE

"Mommy, will you make us a cake, please?"

I have no flour. My pantry is infested with moth-like flies that hitched a ride into our life in a bag of organic brown rice. They lay larva thingies in anything dry.

I haven't made cake in a long time. I moved to a plant-based Nutritarian way of eating last fall and my pantry is just weird. I still haven't found my new normal or established those all important menu staples. So, I have pancake mix and almond flour. Coconut oil and lots of canned beans. Nuts. I have a freezer full of nuts. But, cake, how the heck to make a cake?

Generally, I'd dive into my brain and developed a complicated recipe out of all organic, planty and health friendly ingredients. I'd make health puck 'cookies' or 'nearly cake' mug cake.

For some reason, the way this 4 year old asked for cake...it just got me. Sometimes, sometimes, we just want cake. Real cake. Not a healthy cake. Not some frozen prepackaged excuse for low calorie cake-like substance. Not an imposter. Just straight up cake.

For most cakes - although I totally rock at scratch baking - I prefer to use a cake mix. My kids are sensitive to food colorings though so that has limited the flavors that I'll use. Did you know that chocolate cake mix often contains red #40? Yeah, so, I either do up a spice cake, search labels endlessly for one without color or make a scratch cake.

Today, due to lack of flour, scratch was out of the question. My cake flour looked like an entomologists fantasy and there hasn't been plain flour in this house since Spring.

I opened three boxes of mix. Chocolate. Yellow. Carrot. All seemed ok until I really looked closer. Tiny nasty bugs had eaten through the plastic packages. It's just gross. When I think I've defeated them, I find a new place that they have eluded me.

Finally, I checked the baking cupboard, it's far from the pantry and has remained virgin from the attacks of those nasty little reminders of my organic mishap.

Score! I found a spice cake mix. Only slightly expired.

I insisted on adding fruit and my oldest was upset about this because it wouldn't be plain cake. I finally got him to relent because there would be no frosting. Powdered sugar? Yeah, none of that around here these days.

When this creation came out of the oven my kiddos were so excited. Cake! When was the last time we had cake?!

My 4 year old is so good at sincere authentic compliments. It warms my heart.

"Mmmmmmm. Mommy, you're the best cake maker."

I hugged him and then he went on...

"Mommy, we should keep some cake for daddy when he gets home. He will like it. Remember that cake you made for Papa's birthday that was like this but had apples. Daddy loved that. Mom, this cake is just right. No blueberry cake, no strawberry cake, no berry cake. I just love peach cake. This is the best cake I ever had. I want this kind of cake for my birthday. All the days."

The way my son sat back and savored each bite, closing his eyes and humming... It gave me pause. He was really in the moment. It was a planned enjoyable treat and it was special because we said it was and not because it was just some cake sitting there that needed to be eaten due to obligation of celebration. He just tasted the sweet moments of crumby bliss and that's ok. It's cake. It's not anything else and we ate it. And it was good.

So, what went into this magical cake? Here it is...

Ingredients:

Two cans of peaches packed in water or light syrup

One spice cake mix (whatever the cake mix calls for, 3 eggs, 1/2 cup oil, one cup water)

Two packets of spiced cider drink mix (optional)

A bit less than a 1/2 stick of butter, softened

1/3- 1/2 cup brown sugar (I eyeballed it)

1/2-3/4 cup pancake mix

How to make the cake:

First, preheat the oven to 350F.

Then, dump two cans of peaches into the bottom of an oversized baking dish. Bigger than 9x13 (I used my lasagna dish). Don't drain these babies. You want that juice.

Open up a packet of cider mix and sprinkle it over the peaches. Mmmm, smells so good.

Now, mix up the spice cake by the directions. Mine called for a cup of water, 1/2 cup oil and three eggs. After seeing all that peach water floating around you may want to skimp on the water, don't, we have a plan.

Next, scrape the cake batter out over those lonely peaches. It'll look like it's going to flop. All that liquid. Don't fret, it's going to be great.

Last step, mix the butter, remaining cider mix, pancake mix and brown sugar until crumbly. It won't be a large crumble like the usual streusel topping, part of that topping is going to absorb some of the extra liquid. Sprinkle that magic over the top of the that mess of liquidy goo.

Put it in the oven at 350 (I used 360 due to my oven issues) for 33-38 minutes. I started with 28 minutes and that was definitely not long enough. If it still jiggles in the middle, it's not done. The toothpick trick may not work here if you poke it too far down. You want the cake to be cake, not lava goo. 38 minutes was perfect for mine. I actually poked the center with a knife and looked for the tell tale cake crumb structure. Perfection.

The peaches will still look separate in their liquid. That's how you want it. Serve this with icecream or with a cup of coffee.

This isn't vegan, organic, nutritarian, vegetarian or any other such friendly food. It's just cake. And sometimes, cake is just cake and that is good.

HAPPY

We tell our kids over and over that we just want them to be happy. We do things in order to facilitate that happiness. We try to predict the future by preparing them for it. We push them to fulfill their potential, set and meet goals, achieve, succeed...then, when they grow up with all of this experience and all of these skills, for sure they'll be happy.

Just be happy.

We say we just want our kids to be happy. We feel it in our hearts. We stress and strive and push and contrive. Happy.

What about that?

I think by saying and believing that is all we want we are saying that happiness is a way of being. It's not. It's an emotion, a feeling, as much as sadness. Happiness is a place of being from a space created that generates emotions of happiness. It's like a seed. The seed of emotion doesn't have the capacity to grow without the proper space for cultivation. It's a place of being.

Being in happiness.

If we say we only want them to be happy will they feel shame for having sadness or depression or anxiousness? Would it not be best to say we want them to be. Just be, my sweet child. Just be where you are. Who you are.

Just be Hank. Be Wyatt. Be Ellie.

To be present in whatever place they are and enjoy it or experience it for what it is. And then have the tools and knowledge to let it go and accept what comes next.

Live in the flow of what life brings with honest acceptance and brilliance no matter happiness or sadness. To just be present with themselves and choose their way of being about it.

Wouldn't that be a wish of freedom for them? To have full acceptance of what is and what isn't with the capacity to know the difference and to move through it with ease and fluidity.

Be in happiness.

Be in joy.

Be in the place you are.

Be who you are.

Be. You.

CHOOSE

I had had it. I needed a momcation. I thought of scenes in movies where the mother leaves her family for a weekend and stays at some crappy motel somewhere, just to collect herself. I had to do something. So, I chose. I chose to accept my kids.

Ok, that sounds odd. I love my kids. I really do. They are my heart.

Lately though, I've been feeling myself slip. My warmth abate. My patience has been dwindling and as I felt it nearly dry up and the scratch and sting of unlubricated friction reached a frightening high, yesterday, I caved.

I stood there, in front of the kitchen sink, yelling at my sons to stop yelling. The fear in their faces hit me in the gut. Hard. Yes. It's about as ridiculous as spanking kids for hitting. It was a moment of spiral. A brief glimpse at the life I swore I would never have.

I felt my heart ache for the mother I knew I could be, in those moments, if only I could get a grip. Just get a freaking grip already.

Let it go.

Don't sweat the small stuff.

Goosfrabah.

Whatever the mantra, I've tried it. The one that always comes back to smack me in the face is choose.

Choose.

Choose the people, the situation, the moment for everything that it is and everything that it isn't. In that, the power is yours. Any other way you just stand yelling or whining or complaining, powerless over something that needs little to no manipulation, only choice. Choice to be cause in the matter.

I am cause I'm the matter of how I mother my babies. Yelling. That's me, not them. Losing my temper, my patience, my self... All on me. So, last night as I left the Landmark relationship seminar I've been attending, I chose. I chose to love those little people. And in loving them it would mean that I accept them for everything that they are and everything that they're not.

In making that choice, in accepting that they are just the way they are, and boy, are they so that...it gave me power. I had the power to hand my daughter paper towels to clean up her 5th purposeful spill of the day. I had the power to not freak out as she was grabbing and spilling boiling water off the counter. I had the power to put my phone down and be present with them as they made a river with the hose. I had the power to feed them tea and toast because they thought it sounded fun. I had my power back. I am being the mother I know I'm capable of being.

Today I decided to accept my babies and take back my power as a loving mother and let go of all of the should's and could's and would's. Let go of the control of things being the way they are 'supposed' to be.

It may sound trite but the sky even seems bluer. The grass greener and the air crisper. I feel free. Free to be with them and not judge them and me and every moment against some idea that it's just never going to be as good as it could be. It is what it is and I'm totally ok with all that it is and isn't. Because I have that kind of say.

THINGS MY HUSBAND DOES THAT ARE AWESOME

I'm not a fan of nagging. But I'm not above it. I think I am but the harsh reality of that delusional thinking hits me in the face every single time I open the garbage cupboard door and some piece of refuse tumbles to the floor two days after I asked my loving husband to take the trash out. Run-on sentences are less annoying than that.

I feel the nag rise.

I feel the passive aggressive demon coil in my gut.

And then, I choose. Honestly, most of the time I choose to either take a picture of it and send it to him with a frowny face or make a big show of how fast I can take it out while he stands nearby totally oblivious to the war in my mind. I usually choose that which I'm not proud of.

Why on earth does this matter to me so much?

Every time I take his lack of doing a request personally I wonder about my own sanity. I am a being of light. I am transformed. I am also a freaking hypocrite.

Let's not dwell there though. The purpose of this piece is to shine some light on awareness. Awareness of the helpful things that happen right under our noses that if we can tame the nagging beast we can see some pretty amazing things.

1. I can tell every time my husband uses the vacuum. When he is done he perfectly reattaches each tool and coils the cord exactly as it is meant to be. I, on the other hand, half ass loop the cord around the handle and leave the vacuum in the middle of whatever room I used it with the hose thingy dangling every which way but tidy.

2. He washes windows. Thoroughly. Our windows are pretty gross most of the time but if we have guests coming over, that we don't really know, I will almost always find him with a bottle of cleaner, scrubbing the nose and handprints off each glass surface in our home. I don't remember the last time I washed any window. Really. It's just not on my priority list.

3. He organizes his tools. Now, he often leaves expensive tools out in the weather for long periods of time but, when he does put them away they are like soldiers all lined up and well maintained. When I ask to use a tool, I can always locate it.

4. He has patience with the kids while he does projects. He also includes them. They drag his tools all around and undo his progress over and over and he just takes them by the hand and turns on the hose or gives them a box of clay pigeons to destroy. He will take all three of them to his garage to work on a project so that I can get some cleaning done. His garage, his perfectly tidy garage, usually looks like a natural

disaster hit it when they're done. Does he complain? Nope. Not a word.

5. My husband clips baby fingernails. We currently don't have a baby but he clips all the kids' nails. He's done it since they were days old. I've done it a few times because, well, they grow fast and he has his own nails to clip. But, that man is meticulous. He's only snipped each kid once, and who hasn't snipped the tip of a teeny tiny baby finger at least once. He complains a bit when they are so fresh and new but I know that he kinda likes it.

6. He makes bottles at every feeding, he is there for, when we have a baby. All the night feedings, all the weekend and evening feedings. I breastfeed and he makes a formula bottle. We really had it perfected with the last baby. Breast, breast, bottle. Every time. His support by just making the bottles is what I know played a leading role in my best breastfeeding success yet. My daughter and I had that relationship for 6 whole months because of his help.

7. My hubs is the guy that will lie in bed, while on his phone, and ask if he has clean socks. Yes, it makes me want to throat punch him. He is also the guy that will see the overwhelming pile of laundry and if he has a second to help, he'll toss a load in for me. He usually doesn't say anything about it but I can always tell when he's washed laundry because he takes the time to go from the laundry room to a bathroom and rinse out the soap cup. I leave it all gunky and goopy. When I walk in and the cup is clean, it makes me smile.

There you have it. Although he's been actively working on it, it's true that he's been positively horrible about taking out the garbage in the past. It is on the top ten list of fight starters at our house. But, it's one thing. It's just one thing.

Who cares, besides me and my inner nag?

It is so easy to dwell on the things that annoy us. It is so easy to point out the flaws of those that we know so well. I propose we make a list. Not of the things that piss us off. Set that aside. You can always pick it up later. Write a list of the things that surprise you. The things you'd never do but are so awesome and thoughtful. Write it. Read it. And then, compare it to the pettiness of complaining.

At first, when I started this piece I wasn't sure I could think of 5 things. Then I got to change the title to 7. As I wrote, I realized that I spend so much time complaining in my head about his dirty clothes and boots in the middle of the room and sticky jam on the counters and of course, the garbage, that I haven't spent much time thinking about the good things. The random weird things that no one else would ever know.

No one knows the good stuff. Not even me, until I shine a light on it. Shine that light. It's so worth it.

IT'S NOT EASY

At my youngest son's three year check-up he was supposed to have his vision checked. When my oldest did the check, it was a chart that had shapes and boats and familiar silhouettes. They have since changed the layout of the appointment and they now do the vision check in the room with a book and some weird dinosaur glasses.

Here's where my mom hackles came up, just a little and I became alert. Alert to the medical assistant asking questions and alert to my boys, both of them, and their reactions.

She pulls out the book and says, "Does he know his shapes?"

I didn't want to put him on the spot but was pretty sure he'd been nailing shapes and even drawing and cutting some out of paper.

So, I said, "Sure, most of them. Can you just ask him the ones he knows?"

She then opens the book up to a page with circles, squares, triangles and I don't know what else...And said to my bright and cheery three year old, "Here, these are easy. Let's see what you know."

Right there. There. Blood flushed my face.

Do not tell my child that something is easy. Do not tell my child that something is hard.

Neither is a true statement and are not at all helpful, kind, or in the least bit a contribution to anyone.

He looked and looked and I could see him start to wiggle. He was anxious.

His big brother looked on and whispered encouragement.

He really did know his shapes. I knew he did. I'd seen him point them out with confidence. I'd witnessed him ask about seeing shapes in real life instances.

She pointed to a circle, "This is the easiest one, what is this?"

From my now agitated soon-to-be preschooler, nothing. Squirming.

She pointed to a couple others. I then asked her very directly, "This is a vision test right, not an aptitude test."

Then, I coached, when she just looked at the chart, "Wyatt, is that a circle? Which one looks like a round circle?"

At this, she shut the flip book and said, "Oh, well, it's fine that he doesn't know his shapes, he'll learn them in preschool. We can do the test at his next appointment."

No! No! No!

I screamed in my head. I said nothing as I refuse to make scenes in front of my kids and I couldn't gather myself enough to approach it with grace. No. Please, please don't give up on him with an "oh well..."

The issue here for me is that he could have taken the vision test if coached. Just fine. He could have done it if she would have kept her trap shut about it being easy. He could have done another test with boats and cars and stars and other complicated shit. But, no, she gave up on it for some reason.

My oldest son got a 20/30 on his three year vision test and scored lower on his four year test. His vision got worse. I really wanted that vision test to gage if this second son would also have vision issues. And, I can't for the life of me believe that my three year old is the first and only child to freeze up over shapes.

I've been sitting on this bur under my saddle for over a month now. I've wanted to call the pediatric office and mention it to them and request a vision test with freaking dinosaur pictures and yachts. But, I haven't, still haven't been able to calm down the thunder that built in me.

Does he know his shapes. Hell yes. He also knows numbers and letters and colors and feelings and emotions and social expectations and...I have no idea if he can see properly to learn any more.

Don't give up on little ones. Don't tell them that anything is easy or that it's hard. Those are just stories we make up. Let them learn, grow and shine and encourage it. Wait for them to introduce the concept of difficulty and then coach them through it. That's the best way to learn what they can actually see.

IF YOU REALLY LOOK, ROMANCE IS THERE.

Romance, what is it? I guess that's an age old question that really bears no proper answer. It's an idea made up in the minds of people that need to have something extraordinary to solidify what they already know. It doesn't have to be that way. Romance doesn't have to be with a mate. It doesn't have to be candles and strumming outside a window. It can be whatever you think it is. It can be what you already see without really seeing it.

Where do I find romance?

Romance is when my husband comes home late from work, I feed him warm chicken nuggets, and he takes the kids outside to play by the light of the headlights of his pickup while I clean up. It's in his laugh as he pushes them on the swings and nearly has a seizure due to the flashing of their shadows over the blinding halogen. It's in his joy at watching the three little ones run around in the grass just to show him that they can. It's in the shrill of their giggles as they fall and run and step in dog poop. That's romance.

Romance is holding my daughter's hand at 2am in a full size bed in her room because she is a light sleeper and loves me so much she just wants that extra little bit of me. It's in the way she reaches for my skin to reassure her that there is life right next to her and she is safe. It's right there, in her breath on my arm, while she dreams and my hips and back ache from being in the same position for hours. That is romance.

Romance is waving good-bye to my husband every morning, no matter what we were doing. It's sending him off with joy on our faces although we have clouds in our hearts that he's going. It's there when he turns around after a tearful FaceTime call from one late sleeper that didn't get to wave. It's in that daddy coming back home, just to kiss that snotty sad face and wave one more time. It's in the smile and happiness of that sad little boy knowing just how special he is. That's romance.

Romance is in the way my oldest son touches me mindlessly when he's tired. His little touches and arm strokes remind me of all the tickle touches I've given him over his nearly 5 years of life. It's in those sleep drunk eyes and late night whispers of dreams and hopes. It's when he confides in me that he doesn't want to get old because then I'll get old and that someday he'll have to miss me. That's romance.

Or, romance is watching my son learn how to peel potatoes and enjoying him just soaking up every word his gramma says to him while he takes his new task so seriously. It's in those moments, the everyday, easy-to-miss moments. That's romance.

Romance is in the moments that surprise us. The moments that make our hearts ache with longing for them to last forever. Romance is in the moments that hold ordinary magic, the gas tank he fills before returning the car, the bathroom that smells like pee because another child is potty training, the tiny fingerprints on the freshly cleaned window, eating popcorn for dinner because snuggling kids is more important in that moment than nutrition.

Romance is exactly where you see it and it will never be in a life of someone that is too busy or worried about imaginary ideas to see it.

Romance is there. It's just waiting to be seen, acknowledged and nurtured.

Look. Choose. See.

PAPER AIRPLANES AND RESUMES

I read the other day that we should remove the word irony and ironic from our vocabulary in order to sound smarter. I guess it's an overused word idea that doesn't get used properly. Since I never hear myself use those words it was odd to me to have them pop into my head yesterday.

I'm not one to abide by social cues or norms, and I certainly don't like to be bossed around so, here is the scenario that lead to these thoughts.

I was sitting in a chair, feet up, wearing sweat pants that I am sure have been worn at least four days without a wash. I take them off to sleep, of course, a girl has to have her standards. So, I'm crocheting and watching some Mickey Christmas show on Netflix while the two littlest ones play around my feet. I was having a moment that I often refer to as 'mom zen.'

My oldest child runs in, frantic and out of breath, he hands me a piece of paper. The paper immediately caught my eye. I let out a laugh that even I was surprised by.

He had been looking everywhere for the perfect piece of paper. The best paper available. Not just any paper would do. So, he scoured and searched and after looking high and low he brought me a nice crisp watermarked piece of ecru paper. It was resume paper.

"Mommy, I found the perfect paper for you. Please, please make me a paper airplane. You make them the very best."

Let's just let that settle.

Breath it in.

I expertly crafted him the best paper airplane I could muster out of my old resume paper. Because, well, I'm the best at it. If you don't believe me, see my resume.

FOURTH KID

I've had a few people ask what's different about bringing home our fourth baby. Is it easy or is it hard? What I wonder is how to properly answer such questions. It is what it is. It's different for us than it would be for others and our story is our own, but, here are a few things...

1. You really can do nearly everything with one hand. No, really, washing bottles, disciplining toddlers, going pee, wiping a toddler, reading to little kids, cooking, scrubbing a toilet...pretty much anything.

2. All babies are different. I've had four babies. Each had a very different pregnancy, birth and newborn phase. Each one is different than the last. I anticipate my fourth perfect sweet baby will be no different. At three weeks old, he's already so much his own being.

3. You just do it. Everything. When people say they couldn't do it, that's ridiculous, yes, you can. Lack of sleep, figuring out food, keeping the family in clean clothing, bedtime, breastfeeding while chasing other kids, life. You just do it.

4. The housework seems to be a priority in the little snippets of time when my hands aren't full of baby or helping little people. The matchbox car I'd usually step over gets picked up. The dish on the counter gets loaded into the dishwasher. The laundry gets swapped from the washer to the dryer and then quickly folded. Why is it easier now? It's not, but I realized, ain't nobody got time for this. There will be no chunk of time for tidying. No laundry day. It just must be done whenever possible. It's simply not going to get done if not for bit by bit.

5. I love my husband more. Maybe not more but for sure with more depth. Birthing another human with him by my side, coaching and breathing and encouraging me...watching him jump in and deliver our baby, yet again, there's something so primally appealing about that. This man sees all of what my body goes through to grow, birth and feed these tiny people and he loves me. That there makes him a keeper.

6. Babies are addicting. I'm totally sure that we're done having babies. Kinda. Seriously, I'm 100% positive that my egg makers can be disconnected and then I smell this perfect being. His downy hair tickles my nose. I count his itty bitty toes and I know that my uterus may mutiny if I deny it another occupant. Some people say men think with their genitals. I can say that I may be guilty of thinking with my ovaries. Four is really enough though, probably.

7. People think I'm awesome. I mean that in a totally humble way. Example: I keep being asked if I'm ok and told that I look way too relaxed. I think having a lot of kids, especially all young ones, kind of gives you a get out of anything card. People no longer expect me to be on time or to wear makeup or even to wear real pants. No one at co-op preschool asks me to sign up for anything. And they practically high-

five me for showing up. Not that it's not commendable to even leave the house after not sleeping and dealing with a circus of monkeys I birthed myself. It is but I'm not the only mom with more than three little ones.

8. Sleep deprivation is subjective. What is actual sleep deprivation. I have had fewer than ten full nights of sleep in the last five years. So, I thought it wouldn't be a big deal to wake up a few more times. Let me tell you, I was wrong. I'm running on a mere few hours of sleep for the last four weeks and I can tell my sanity is unraveling. I only thought I was sleep deprived before. Now, 5 hours of sleep would be a dream.

9. Pro status isn't all it's cracked up to be. When I was in the hospital and a partner of my OB rounded on me for discharge, he said, 'Well, with 4 kids you've reached pro status so you know all this...' I don't remember what else he said because I was busy being proud of myself and then wondering what I already knew. Pro status may or may not be a thing but it doesn't make it any less tiring or scary or unspecial to bring home a new baby. It doesn't make the cramping and bleeding and nursing and sleepless nights and hormones any less real. It just makes it more familiar. And it reminds me that it's not forever; it's fleeting.

10. I am desperately aware of how short the newborn, infant and littleness stage is. I sit just a little longer. I smell him one more time before putting him down. I am patient when I used to be frantic. I see him changing and growing every day, and though my heart aches with the permanence of the forward momentum, I know that life just moves into another phase.

DISTRACTION

Some days I catch myself, curled up, soaking in information, deep inside my phone. I crawl in and numb out the world. Scroll, scroll, click, follow trail, more information, must take in more information... hungry to fill a void, aching to hide from the breathing, noisy, living world.

I haven't quite pinned it down but I am present to it. Today is one such day. A couple hours have passed and I've put my phone down several times, only to pick it up again and climb back in.

It's usually when I feel disconnected or I'm looking for answers. It's usually when I'm on the verge of learning another piece of a puzzle. It's usually when I'm emotionally spent or physically exhausted or, avoiding something. It's usually not usual. It's just a phone. It's just me. It's just something that has become a habit. Habits are meant to be replaced.

Today, I replace this habit, if only for today, with tidying, movie time with babies and, crochet.

Because, because.

I FORGOT HOW TO MOM

We spent 6 days away from our three Littles. At first I just missed their little voices and snuggles. Then, as the days became more enjoyable and I became more comfortable just being with my husband and being me again I really started to come apart and reassemble. I began to let go. I began to forget how to mom.

Before we left for vacation things were rough. I was snappy and short with the kids and my husband and everyone was becoming more and more defiant and emotional. I was numb and even - I hate to admit this - cold and uncaring. My attitude toward my sweet family was one of survival. Just meeting their basic needs and getting through the day. I'd lie in bed at night dreading my little girl's night wake ups and cries and crying over how much it hurt me to feel so out of control. I'd see the nasty looks on my sons faces and know that I was really just seeing a mirror of my own reactions to them. I'd read blog posts about being more mindful and positive and I'd try and fail to be the good mother, the warm happy mom. I felt like I was drowning.

The night before we left for our Maui vacation I sat in the kid's bed at my in-laws, between my two struggling little boys. They were fighting sleep and fighting it hard. I sat there feeling hopeless and sad and horrible. I scratched their tiny backs and tickled their skin like they asked. I felt frustration boiling inside. Why had things gotten this bad? Why wouldn't they just sleep so I could sleep and get the hell out of there to paradise? Their breath became rhythmic and the gentle sounds of their bodies giving in to sleep became a song. The song pierced my aching cold heart and the dam broke. I bawled. This, this was paradise. I just wasn't seeing it. I wasn't appreciating it. I wasn't living it. I lived it like it was a prison and in doing so that is what my life as a mother and wife had become.

I snuggled up to my middle child and willed him to feel my warmth. My imagination ran away with my emotions and I pictured myself dying in some tropical mishap or our plane going down. What would my babies remember of me? My snappy demands. My callous retorts to their neediness. Would they know how much I love them? Would they know how badly I regretted every day I saw their hearts sink because of some failure of my patience or abilities? Would they remember the warmth of my beating heart beneath their sleeping baby cheeks during late night feedings?

We all die. The irony is that we live like we won't. What would my mothering legacy teach my kids? I vowed right then, as I cried into my sleeping child's hair, that I would reset, restart and relearn what it means to be a mother. I would forget how to mom and start from a place of 'I miss you, I love you' when I returned from vacation instead of my previous place of 'what do you want now.' I would be present to their needs, present to their light, acknowledge them in everything they are and are not and choose to love them all the ways possible.

This morning is our first day together back at our home and I'm successfully learning how to mom.

MOM GUILT: CONFESSIONS

There are many legitimate reasons for mom guilt. Like, thousands. There are lists of horrid parenting fails to elicit audible gasps from the peanut gallery. Yes, I'm guilty. Perhaps I should elucidate.

Parenting confession número uno:

When I hear screams I don't run to the rescue. I often don't even walk. Let's be honest here, with three kids, unless there's blood or a compound fracture, it's going to be ok. Even a trip to the emergency room or a call to poison control isn't that big of deal. I know *gasp* but seriously, I have most sharp objects out of reach, there are no corrosive or caustic chemicals just lying around and I'm relatively alert to the whereabouts of my minions. If there is screaming, I listen. Just as I have identified the different barks of my dogs I know the screams and cries of my Littles. I can tell if there is frustration, distress (as in, 'I'm stuck') or pain. My instincts are rarely off in this sense and so I listen, evaluate the need for my presence and often wait for a report from a tattling toddler. No one has ever died or been severely injured on my shift so, mom fail admitted.

Parenting confession number two:

My husband and I still sometimes lie in bed with our 4 and 2 year olds until they fall asleep. No, I don't care to fight with them and get drinks of water or deal with late night sneaking. Sometimes it's just easier to lie there and tickle their backs and sniff their dirty little kid hair until sleep takes the little monsters away and leaves sweet baby angels. Guilty. I don't care.

Parenting confession number three:

My house is a pit. Well, I shouldn't be so harsh. It's not always a crumb covered sticky mess of piled dishes, muddy foot prints, laundry mountains and urine odor in every bathroom...except when it is. I have spent hours, days, weeks, months and years of my life worrying about my housekeeping abilities and how they define me. The truth is, they don't. My kitchen is rarely clean for two consecutive days and I'm okay with that. I clean the bathrooms once a week and by day 3 they smell like my boys don't even try to hit the bowl. I wash a load of dishes daily but often forget to unload it and end up missing a day and that creates a pile. I try to wash, dry and put away a load or two of laundry daily and that often results in washing the same soured load three times because front load energy efficiency also means 'good luck washing your clothes with three cups of water and the perfect recipe for mildew'. Yes, this ends up creating yet another backup. The bedrooms have dirty clothes and toys and odd kitchen utensils strewn about. The playroom is such that it appears that it was tidied with a shotgun cannon stuffed with toys and the common areas appear to be organized by a person with a goldfish's attention span. Whatevs. We live in it and it doesn't kill us. Just call two days before you come over if you want to visit the tidy version of our home.

Parenting confession number four:

I used the Ferber Method for sleep training my first born at 6 months old. We set timers and did the graduated absence and we cried while he cried and in one night at one minute increments he finally went to sleep with puffy eyes and a tear soaked sheet at the 7 minute mark. I regret that but he seems to be no worse for wear...except that he is my worst sleeper, has horrible night terrors and ends up in my bed at least 3 nights a week. But, who doesn't eff up something big with their first born? Not that it's right but I am comforted in knowing that we didn't go full on cry it out and that we really did and do respond to every cry and wake up after the initial Ferberizing transpired.

Parenting confession number five:

My last two babies have routinely fallen asleep with a bottle, in their bed, and I let them. To be fair, a toddler (16 months old) with a bottle, so it's kind of a double fail. My first two were free of their bottles at 11 and 10 months and they did it on their own. The last tiny human snuggles down on her pillow (yes, she also has a pillow *gasp*) wraps her arm around her soft baby doll or her stuffed elephant and props her bottle up on her fluffy blankie and hums and coos and jabbers while she slurps down 8oz. of toddler formula bliss.

My pediatrician would wail. I even lie when I check the box on the intake form...

Q: Do you put infant to bed with a bottle?

A: Nope!

She's never had an ear infection and I brush her teeth. I'd rather deal with whatever ailment bottle sleeping will cause than the trouble resulting from sleep training. Call me paranoid. No effing way am I going to set a timer for my last baby to cry herself to sleep. I don't care when she gives up the bottle or how long she takes to sleep through the night. It's just not worth the trouble and emotional baggage for me.

Parenting confession number six:

Sometimes when the angels become monsters and I know that a healthy snack isn't going to happen, I just feed them peanut butter from the jar. They stand in front of me like baby birds, their mouths gaping and their chirps of hunger grating my nerves in all of their carnal cuteness. I spoon in globs of creamy bliss and watch them, like dogs, try to maneuver it around their mouths. After a couple spoons and a glass of water we are generally all in a better mood and the silliness of eating peanut butter sets the tone moving forward. It's a weird kind of reset and it works for us.

Parenting confession number seven:

I give grandparents free rein. I only have a couple rules...

No red #40, yellow #5, #7 or #11
No aspartame, msg or carrageenan and
No corporal punishment or yelling at my children

Other than these few requests I don't care what my kids are allowed to do at their grandparents. I don't remember ever dying from eating ice cream for breakfast or from staying up too late or from watching a PG 13 movie at my grandparents house. I do remember feeling like, although they had rules, grandparents were awesome and a much needed break from parents. I want my kids to have relationships with their grandparents that happen organically and that are comfortable and awesome and full of memories that are as unique as our parents.

My rules aren't more important than that.

I'm not a bit ashamed of myself for these things. I do what works for us. I do my best and I cut corners where I can. It is what it is. I have enough mommy guilt from using my phone too much, hiding in the closet to eat chocolate or from not doing enough learning activities with the kids. I'm comfortable failing in some areas so I can own a few huge wins. I encourage you to share your 'fails' with other moms. We're human. Sharing our humanity is what bring us together, not how we parent.

THE TRAINING WHEELS ARE OFF

I knew this day would come. I hadn't put much thought into preparing for it as I've learned that preparing for the inevitable is a lot like trying to wash windows with a messy toddler nearby. It's just a silly time waster.

The day we gave the sweet little toddler the shiny red glider bike and he wobbled around and crashed and cried, I knew the rumors were true; you really can't stop these beings from growing up and they do it at a speed that is both uncomfortable and achingly points to our own mortality. His Gramma B gave him that glider bike and he kicked and scooted his way all over the driveways with it for two summers. It was scratched up, beat up and the tires were nearly bald by the time it was passed down to his little brother last summer. He was so proud to give it to him though.

At first it took some coaxing. We had to assure him that the glider was for little boys like his then nearly two year old brother. His new glossy big boy bike, from Gramma C was for big boys like him. He warmed up pretty fast. Our one mistake was not removing the training wheels prior to presenting him with it. He had established astute balance from the glider and was ready to try the big boy bike but when we started removing the training wheels he threw a tantrum. The tantrum was disappointment, fear and utter despair that his beautiful big boy bike was being disassembled.

Because he received the bike with 4 wheels he really thought that it just had to have all of those wheels to be a whole functioning bicycle. So, all last Spring and Summer, he rode that bike. He road fast and hard and confidently. My husband and I were convinced that we had ruined his equilibrium and his chance at riding a big boy bike sans training wheels was over forever. Dramatic, but, hey, he's our first born. Everything about the first born is a little over the top.

Recently, my uncle sent us a photo of a tiny motorcycle that he had taken in trade for some product (he sells Snap-on tools). He gave us an open invitation for Hank to come ride it whenever he wanted. When we showed the photo to him, he was over the moon excited. The one caveat was that he had to learn to ride his bike without the extra little wheels. He agreed that he'd do it. And so the conversations and lead up began. This weekend we were presented with amazing weather and so my husband declared that it was time to remove the little wheels.

As I watched my husband hold the back of the little bike and the little boy hold on with confidence and fear, my heart grew loud in my ears. My husband jogged a bit and Hank held the handlebars steady. After a bit, his dad let go and he just kept going. There was no wobble, no stumble, no crash. He just sat up straight in the seat and pedaled in his brand new cowboy boots and rode. I had anticipated it being more. I had imagined it being less. I thought it would be crashing and crying and scrapes and bruises. I thought I'd have time to prepare my heart for the jerk and ache of watching my first born, my baby boy, ride away from me with the most important facet of freedom in one's childhood. I just thought I'd have time to rub the sting out of my eyes before hearing him ride straight and true yelling, "I'M DOING IT! I'M DOING IT!"

The rest of the day was riding bikes. The original glider bike met it's demise last fall when I ran over it with my unforgiving SUV. We hid it from our poor little W. Their Gramma C had just gotten them bells for the handlebars and everything. Total bummer. Fortunately, I was able to find one on Lightning Deal on Amazon during Winter and, as my husband knew that removing training wheels would be a big deal and possibly overshadow the little brother, he assembled the brand spanking new red glider (same model) and presented it to our younger son. The two boys rode up and down the dirt driveways all day. They also slept like rocks.

Today, Hank said to me that he will have to practice a little bit more before he can ride my uncle's motorcycle but that he's a big boy and practicing is how he'll get better. My 4 year old that hides and insists he can't do most new things has found something he's passionate about and the world of scrapes and falls won't stop him from achieving his goal. He'll be a big boy on a motorcycle.

SPRING AND THE UNEXPECTED

Every year since we've lived out here on the scab rock and clay I've waited excitedly for spring. The first spring, I waited more than excitedly, it was more like freakish anxiousness. I wanted to burn our house down that year, from cabin fever, and all I could think of was getting out of it and into some sunshine and dirt.

That first spring I had a tiny baby boy on my hip and I was mostly terrified to leave the house with him. You know, babies combust in the sun and vanish in shopping carts. I mostly made napping a newborn an excuse to watch seasons of shows on Netflix that first year. I had to hold him or he wouldn't nap. I couldn't exactly expect a tiny baby to nap on my chest in the fresh air and sun. So, we kind of skipped over that whole first spring and into the summer.

To be honest, I was in such a new mom haze I don't rightly remember much of my son's first year of life. Well, I remember small pieces of important things and special moments but I have no idea what our days were like. What did we even do in those hours out here alone while my husband worked and the world moved on around us. I have no real recollection.

I do remember the second spring. I was plump with child and busy with a sweet perfect amazing toddler. We went for walks looking for flowers and sticks and rocks and puddles. We threw the ball for the dog and built roads in the driveway for tiny cars and tractors. We played in the dirt. We built forts with the patio furniture and we soaked up everything about living out in the freedom of dirt and rocks and trees.

That spring, my oldest and then only son, would grab tiny delicate flowers with his fists and smash them into my hand. Mostly his dad would encourage him to bring me delicate things, matted and squished by his tiny chubby hands. I remember his short fingers desperately trying to pinch flowers and get them to me as his daddy cheered him on. Mostly, my gifts were rocks. Rocks don't get crumpled in eager little hands. I kept a few here and there.

By the third spring I was getting into my mom groove. I had a full on toddler and a sweet new baby and we were ready for adventure. By this time my first born knew about flowers but had no real interest in picking them without provocation. I have a few sweet memories of him out on the back of the property with my mother. They were in their own world just exploring and pointing and picking and poking at the world. None of this has anything really to do with where I intended to go with this piece but it's quite interesting to me how one small happening can open a floodgate of memories and emotions.

When our first kid was born it was all my husband and I could do to anticipate his next milestone. It was very much the same as hating winter only a few days after the cold sets in. The rest of the dreary months get spent wishing for sun and spring and grass. Our perfect little boy was nothing like winter but we could barely live in what was with the promise of what would be right there too. He was advanced, of course, he was gifted and a damn genius. All first children are, aren't they?

I feel as though we wished his precious tininess away. His crushing of the flowers, his eagerness to toss them over his shoulder in order to get a stick or rock that was way better than giving his mother a piece of squished dead plant. We pushed him and encouraged him and videoed and photographed every step not realizing we really were missing something huge. The second baby and then the third really brought that all into perspective. It's just so fleeting. Like spring, when we realized we are in it it's almost given way to the heat of summer.

Everyone says to enjoy them when they're small. Let the house be dirty. Let the laundry pile up. No one really says anything about the guilt that comes with wishing it away. Pining for the day they will feed themselves, sleep through the night, wipe their own butts, get their own toast, go to school.

This is it.

This is the life. This is the time that I'll look back on while yacking my daughter-in-law's ears off about her husband when she has their baby. These are the moments that I'll cry about with longing when my kids are all in their rooms as teens and I have no one to really need me. It's hard. It's lonely. It's a daily struggle to not yell and be irritated and just wish it all away.

I know this.

It haunts me. I have flashes of each of my three babies at my breast and now they are just breasts. I stuff them in a bra without a thought. There was a time that the world revolved around them. I didn't savor it enough. I didn't appreciate that enough.

Today, my oldest boy went adventuring and brought me two of the first flowers of spring. Buttercups. Sweet smelling, delicate tiny incarnations of the first vestiges of sunshine. He brought them to me on his own. He told me how beautiful and delicate and amazing they are. He then went back and got a handful and after that he took a plastic box out and filled it with every last buttercup he could find and delivered it to me with such awe, wonder and ceremony that I almost burst into tears.

His hands are getting longer and stronger and yet they don't crush the crepe thin petals. He articulates his observations about them like a tiny poet. I no longer even think about the next milestone. I no longer wonder what he'll do next.

They are all so different and do things at their own pace and I'm just here wishing we could move a little slower. Stay a little longer. Just savor the smell of these sweet flowers, the sound of their voices, the chill in the air and stay in spring for just a little bit longer. Stay in this fresh and new and wondrous time of our lives.

PART 3

SECRETS ARE MEANT TO BE SHARED

"The thing is, when
you cut those tethers,
those safety lines,
what happens is
incredible. When you
aren't held back,
held down, holding on...

You fly."

WOLF AND MAN

Last night I dreamed that I was supposed to kill a wolf. I tried to strangle it and crush it's windpipe with my knees and my hands and it just wouldn't die. It's eyes begged to be seen. I was so consumed with killing it that I didn't realize it had turned into a man.

I don't know what he said as he spoke to me but his words and the look in his eyes made me feel a deep compassion for him. My heart ached because I knew I was still supposed to kill him. He sat up on a chair and we talked for a long time. But I still had this feeling that I was supposed to kill him and this voice kept telling me to do so. Out of compassion for the man and anger for the guilt I felt, I turned to confront the voice telling me to kill.

The man reached out and took my hand.

As I turned my attention to the voice I didn't notice the man had turned back into a wolf. The hand I held in mine turned to a paw. As I felt the fur under my fingers my heart sank. Before I could turn to see the animal I felt its teeth sink into the flesh of my arm. I released it's paw and it ran away without looking back.

I've pondered this today.

There's something I've been avoiding for years and tonight I will confront it.

A beast.

A beast that I thought for a long time that I must kill. The beast is a man. The man deserves compassion. In seeking to feel a deep compassion for this being I have dredged up innumerable questions.

My take away from this... A wolf is a wolf.

Even wolves deserve compassion. Compassion makes them no less beastly but it isn't our purpose to do so. It isn't our place to decide if they are beast or man. Peace and compassion remove the beasts facade and reveal the being that hides deep, shuddering, hoping for redemption.

Man and beast are one; it just depends on who is looking.

I DID THE IMPOSSIBLE

I did the impossible. This is a story of how a Landmark Education Program gave me the tools to uncover my super powers.

At the moment I have a twisted knot in my gut and a lump in my throat. My cheeks are hot and my upper lip is prickling with sweat. The hammering of my heart threatens to dislodge the lump in my throat and send it hurtling through my body, an embolism hell bent on my destruction.

One year ago on this day I woke up a new person. I opened my eyes on a new world, endless possibilities and complete and utter relief. I woke up relaxed and in love with life. My heart felt free and rested, as if it had spent decades beating itself against iron bars and suddenly it was being cradled in loving hands, my hands, with my compassion. For the first time in years the deafening static in my mind was hushed and I felt peace.

I said I would write about it. I said I would share it with the world. I made a commitment to myself and to millions of suffering people. I was going to, I wanted to, and then time happened. I waited to talk to this person or that person and I waited for the time to be right.

The thing is, there is no right or wrong time to tell the world some things. There is only time, pain, suffering and the promise of enlightenment and peace.
That's it, no pressure.

A year ago today I woke up and felt completely free because I had done something I felt was entirely impossible. I had met, face to face, with my childhood sexual abuser. I met with him and I found peace in the conversation that started with me taking responsibility for the story of my life. I sat across from him as he white knuckled a cup of coffee and I treated him like a person. I spoke to the person that sat in front of me. I didn't see the man of the past. I created a space of peace and I did the unthinkable…I invited him to step into it.

How?

Why?

What. The. Hell.

I know. It seems completely insane but even as I share this I know there are so many people that will be triggered by it. There will be hate, fear, nausea, confusion, self doubt, sadness. So, as best as I can I will share something that transformed my life.

When I completed the Landmark Forum in October of 2014 I had no idea I would be tackling such a monumental task. I learned some tools that helped me understand myself and humanity. I skimmed the surface

of what was possible for me but deep inside my being I held on to this
story. I held onto my pain. I protected my right to feel or act any way I
wanted because I was entitled to it. I was a victim of the most socially
accepted kind. I had been sexually abused, molested, raped. Who could
tell me I needed to let go of that? So I didn't. I made connections, I
paraded my new bright happiness around and puffed out my Landmark
transformed chest.

It worked for a while. I was able to superficially exist in a space of
possibility but never fully embraced being 100% responsible for my
life. I didn't understand the concept of being cause in the matter of my
entire existence. Now, this, this distinction is where it gets dicey.

A few months passed and I was enrolled in another Landmark program,
a seminar offered to Forum graduates. It was a conversation expanding
on the tools and distinctions we learned in the Forum. For 9 weeks I
experienced amazing things. I watched as other seminar participants
had breakthrough after breakthrough. The more I witnessed these
people getting free of their constraints, letting go of their pasts, owning
their part in the creation of what was possible for them, the more I
festered and became aware of my own stories.

At the 10th session, the last in the seminar series, I sat at the front
of the room, agitated and restless. My knee bounced, my palms were
clammy. I had to figure out how I was right and how I could get free
while still holding on to the story that had both buoyed and drowned
me throughout my life.

The seminar leader was out of sorts. She paced and the cadence of
her voice was off, jerky. She looked and sounded like I felt. Then,
something happened. She stood on the stage and she shared that she
found an incompletion in her life. She realized that she was incomplete
with a rape that happened when she was 18. My heart slammed into my
rib cage. The humming in my ears turned to searing heat. I slid to the
edge of my seat. I tried to quiet the roar in my head.

She stood there naked, bare and on the verge of something great. Her husband, a retired Forum Leader, stood at the back of the room and watched the beauty of his wife blossom as she peeled back one more layer of her soul. My focus was on what I wanted to hear. I expected her to say there was no way to be responsible for such a horrible thing. I expected validation. Something I've sought my whole life. I listened for her to make a stand for every victim that ever hushed their pain and stuffed down their worth.

What she said sent me into a near rage. She stood there and said that what she realized she needed to get complete was to take responsibility for what happened. She had to take responsibility for the story she lived in around what happened. She had to be cause in the matter of her life.

No. No. No.

Impossible.

Victims aren't responsible for what happens to them. Victims are entitled, deserving, raised up to a higher status than the rest. Victims have something. Victims have their story. I had mine. It was precious to me. It fueled every single context I moved inside of in my life. I needed it. Without it…what would I be without it?

The conversation started to move on and I was crawling out of my skin. I shot my hand up to share, to ask, to prove that it wasn't possible to get complete with rapists. Bad guys are bad guys. Period.

I'm not sure if she called on me or if she was trying to dismiss me to move on with the discussion but I stood up. I walked to the microphone and I looked into the eyes of over 100 people. I looked at the first people that would know my story. Besides that moment I had only told 5 people.

I wiped my hands on my pants and clenched my jaw. As I asked my question I saw something flicker in the leader's eyes and then they welled up. She sat down and her husband stood up.

"How do you take responsibility for being raped, sexually abused, and molested when you are a child? How can a 6 year old be cause in the matter of that kind of horrible thing? Tell me. Tell me how is it possible to get complete with that?!"

I stood there, my teeth ready to crumble under the pressure of my tightening jaw. I stared daggers into the retired Forum leaders eyes. I dared him to challenge me. Begged for him to try and prove me wrong. There was no answer to that kind of question. A victim is always right.

He took a breath and looked at his wife, she sat folded up and crumpled, white and shrunken in her director's chair. Then he looked back at me and said something I will never forget.

"You can't. You can't get complete with something like that because there's always going to be a bad guy for you. As long as there's a bad guy you will always be the judge, the jury, you'll always be right. As long as you're always right you'll always be a victim. As a victim, you don't have to get complete."

I hated him. I wanted to light him on fire. I wanted to crush every bone in his lie spitting face. Who in the hell was he to call me out and strip away the one thing that held me together?! Without my story, without the power of being the victim, I was nothing.

I stood shaking and speechless. I wanted it to be easy. I wanted it to be what I wanted. I wanted, no needed, to be right.

Then he prodded, "Right? You just have to be right. You have to have a bad guy. There's always a bad guy for you and you decide who is bad. You think that gives you power but all it does is leave you a victim of the bad guy. You're always the victim. Right? Right?!"

I breathed in. I breathed out. In the moment between two breaths something happened. I heard a gurgling, a crackle. I felt heat and tingling and rushing of blood and adrenaline. The drums in my ears reached a deafening pitch and then as if a roaring fire was suffocated so the din of my being was silenced. In the space between two breaths I became present to something. I felt something open up and I saw for the first time in 26 years that I had a part to play and it wasn't as a victim.

The tears came and what poured out of my mouth was no longer tinged with righteous indignation. I spoke of my responsibility. I spoke of my sisters, my mother, my husband and last of all, my self. I got present to the story I had been living in, rueing in, suffering in. I got present to what that created for anyone close to me. I bled. I ached. A union of both release and the utter ripping apart of the fabric of who I thought I was.

Then, I sat down.

As I drove home that night I was alive. I felt electric. I had to get complete with all of these loved ones. I had to give my sisters peace and my blessing to love their dad. I had to let my mom know that I didn't blame her for what had happened. I had to write it all down. I had to share.

Over the next few months I did just that. I met with my step dad's two daughters, my sisters, and took responsibility for the story I had lived in and the power it had over their entire childhood and life. I apologized for them not being able to love their dad because of the fear they had of how that would impact me. I cleaned that wound out with medical grade precision. And then I kept moving. Action, always in action. I went down my list until finally I came to the second to last person I had to get complete with. My step dad. The abuser.

I called my youngest sister and enrolled her in the possibility of me actually meeting with her dad. I asked her to bring him to meet me in a public place. I asked out of love and when fear rose up I karate chopped it in the repulsive face.

The night that the meeting had been arranged for I was numb. I had enrolled several people in supporting this meeting so that I couldn't back out. I hadn't figured out what I was going to say or how in the hell I was going to separate my responsibility with the actual actions of this man so many years ago. I didn't have it all plotted out and I didn't want to. I wanted to feel it, be it, have it organically sprout up from authenticity and the integrity of a commitment I had made at my Landmark Forum.

At my Forum I had created the possibility of being compassion, love and kindness for the world. I had no idea what that meant when I declared it but it had finally come full circle. I had to set the bad guy free and allow space for him to exist as what and who he is now and relinquish the hold on my story of what he was and what it meant about me.

As I stepped out of my vehicle and stared at the pub that would be our meeting place, I felt a bit lost without the security of expectation and fear. But, it felt good. It felt incredible. It felt powerful.

I crossed the street and heard my sister call my name. I had assumed they would already be inside and I would be approaching a table, two seated individuals and the key to my future of unhindered living. I didn't expect to see him walking toward me. I didn't expect to feel complete peace as he approached.

The street lights played shadows across his form. I knew him before the glow lit his face and then danced its way into darkness. I knew this man from long ago. But it wasn't what I once saw. The man that walked toward me looked scared, he looked ashamed, he walked weakly like a dog knowing it was about to be beaten. This wolf of a man, the nightmare that plagued my innocence like a rotting disease, eating away the flesh of my being, was rendered helpless in my presence.

In an instant we were face to face. I had hugged my sister with joy and at the moment of letting go, there he was. His eyes were empty, searching, sadness, black in the hollows of the dim blinking orbs. I had imagined this moment for so many years. What I would say. What physical violence I would wage on his aged body. I had imagined it, played it out, rehearsed and solidified another story. And yet, there I stood, smiling.

I looked at him, searching his eyes for the child within his soul that had been hurt long ago. I peered in and saw his humanity, the truth that we are all whole and complete beings and it's just one story, one happening, one fucking trauma from completely coming undone. I saw him. I saw his worth as a human, his shame as a man, I saw it all. And it felt amazing.

I said, "Hi, how are you?"

With those four words he seemed to be both destroyed and resurrected. There was something that flashed in his eyes and I think it was surprised relief.

We all walked into the pub and my sister went and sat at the bar. My step dad and I sat at a table and the waitress stood poised for our order. Coffee. He only wanted coffee.

I waited a few minutes. I just sat silently smiling, a freaking zen statue of all the things I'd never imagined possible. I'm sure I must have been glowing because as he looked across the table at me, he squinted just a little.

The next hour passed in a moment. I broke the beginning silence with a short and true statement.

"I have something to say to you and it isn't anywhere close to anything you may have imagined."

And then, I went on as he held his coffee cup, knuckles white, palms slipping on the ceramic. I explained that I acknowledge there was abuse. I know and remember it all. Every single moment and heart wrecking detail. What I was there for wasn't to hash it all out and rub his nose in how horrible a person he was.

I started with explaining my completion with his daughters and how I was sorry that he didn't get to have the relationship that may have been possible with them over the years. I told him how the story I built about what the abuse meant about me had impacted all the relationships and decisions in my life. I became cause in the matter of my suffering, my fear and my story.

Lastly, I told him that I now see him as a whole and complete human and that I no longer live inside the story of victimhood or believe that what happened has any meaning about my worth. Then, a power washed over me. Something descended upon my being. It was quick and it was complete. Not only did I feel peace but I felt love.

Oh, now, I know this is the part where so many people will pretty much shit their pants. I get it. I've been there. Light him on fire, cut off his dick, peel off his skin and cover him with ants. Really, I get that. I'm telling you right in this moment, you have to step outside of whatever meaning you're living in and just be present with me… just a little bit longer - I felt love for a human being, love for humanity, compassion and hope for every person on the planet because in that moment I didn't have to be the judge anymore.

The real power came when I enrolled him in a new possibility for himself. I enrolled him in the possibility that in the current moment he too could let go of the story he had created for himself. He could step out of the bonds of shame and crippling regret and be whole and complete. His story didn't have to be real anymore or ever.

And he cried.

When I left the pub I was new. I can't honestly put into words what raced through my head in the 20 minute drive home. It was close to midnight when I walked into my bedroom and my husband was in a cold sweat. The dam broke in me and I shared all the beauty I never expected to unfold in the meeting.

On this day a year ago I started something, I set something in motion and the ripples of that one gesture, that single conversation, have traveled farther than I'll ever know. Since that evening I have had the pleasure of being a stand for my step dad to complete his Landmark Forum and in that space he has transformed his life in ways that even he doesn't quite understand.

The last name on my completion list was my dad. I had to get complete with keeping my abuse a secret from him for 26 years. I had to tell him that the man he trusted to care for his daughters had actually abused me. I waited. I waited. And, I waited. I had a story about my dad. The story went something like this... My dad always said he'd kill anyone that ever touched his daughters. I never told him about it because I didn't want him to go to prison. Even after all the powerful things I'd completed I still held him as unable to comprehend where I was coming from.

I finally invited him up, for a visit with the intention of coming clean. We walked around a pond by my house and I just blurted it all out. All of it. This whole story came bubbling out. Then I stood there and watched his face.

It was magical. Because I had come from a place of compassion and forgiveness the story hit him on a completely different level. He surprised me and I think he surprised himself. And just like that, 26 years of built up 'what ifs' was dissolved.

Freedom.

I can hear the questions and objections now. I know them all so it's not necessary to hash them out. Save it. Put that energy into the complete impossibility that everything we can imagine is possible.

I invite you to try on the possibility that everything that creates that gut ball and searing hate is actually fear. Fear that if the story is gone, the bad guy is just a guy, and we have to step up and own all the stuff we put out into the world, we will fall. The thing is, when you cut those tethers, those safety lines, what happens is incredible. When you aren't held back, held down, holding on…

You fly.

HE LEFT MY SHOES ON

Today I am present to an incidence of sexual abuse. It was not my previous occurrence of abuse, it was a neighbor boy, he was 4 years older than me. I think it was close to the time I learned to ride a bike.

We arrived and their kitchen smelled of coffee. They had an old fashioned wood stove, with a camp coffee pot perking. The heat was intense. The window above the sink was half open. The boy, was building a blanket fort in his room. I was told to go play. He invited me in and closed the bedroom door.

We played for a while and then he asked me to take off my pants. I didn't want to but he told me our moms said that he was in charge of me and I had to do what he said. I felt fear. He told me again that I had to take off my pants. They were corduroy and a bit thick and awkward to get off. I pulled them down awkwardly. He tugged them off over my shoes.

He left my shoes on.

He got a flashlight out of his dresser and came back into the fort. I felt cold and scared. He shined the light in my eyes and I felt my face get hot as white spots covered my vision. I felt his hands fidgeting with my panties. He pulled at them and shined his flashlight onto my body. He told me to take them off. I didn't. He pushed me back and took them down and left them, like a hobble, at my shoes.

They were fabric Mary Janes. I looked down and white spots blurred over where I knew an embroidered rose was stitched into the top of the toe covering. He pulled my legs up and as my feet came nearer my face, I could make out the intricacies of the threads in the stitching on the petals.

I felt his fingers, searching, prodding, curious. I felt hot and numb. I could hear our mother's voices and I wondered why they would let this happen. I wondered why the pain I felt, as fingers moved inside my body, was somehow aloud because I was little and he was big.

He shined the light onto his exploration and then, as quickly as it started, he was in my face. He had pulled down his pants and his genitals were so close to me that I couldn't make out the detail of the wad of skin.

He told me to touch him because it was only fair. He had touched me and now it was my turn. I didn't know how I should touch him. I rubbed at him and watched him grow and get firm. He rubbed into me.

He said that if he put his parts inside my parts that we would make a baby together so we couldn't do that.

Our mothers called for him to clean up our mess and for me to come out when we were done. He handed me my pants and I pulled up my panties and took off my shoes to put on my pants.

He asked me if I knew what secrets were. He explained that this was our secret and that we're friends and that friends have these secrets.

I left the room and went to my mother. She scolded me for not having my shoes on. I couldn't adjust the buckles. The latch was too cumbersome. I cried. She scolded me for crying about my shoes.

PART **4**

NO ONE TALKS
ABOUT THIS STUFF

"It doesn't matter. None of it matters. I'm going to die some day. All those excuses will die right along with all the words I never wrote, all the experiences I never shared. The smiles and hugs I didn't give. All of it, gone."

NO ONE TALKS ABOUT THIS STUFF

There's so much to being a parent, an adult, a freaking human. So much that happens behind the scenes, under the surface or just doesn't seem news worthy.

I'm finding that it is in those moments, often grueling and even fleeting, that I look around me and wonder how anyone makes much sense of it.

How do I reconcile the times when I love all of my children but want to toss that one to the wolves because the safety or sanity of the whole seems far more important.

How do you tell a coworking that you were pregnant yesterday but today you're not and there's nothing to show for it but the dull emptiness in your eyes when someone says the word baby.

I often imagine what goes on behind the smiles of strangers that pass me in the grocery store. I make up elaborate histories for panhandlers and prostitutes. I wonder if there was more humanity in conversations about 'how we're doing' if people would make different choices for themselves.

Or, maybe, maybe it's just that I'm weird and feel lonely when I'm yelling at my kids for the 5th time on the day I swore that yelling was done in our home.

Whatever it is, nobody really talks about it.

SHARE THE NEWS IF YOU WANT TO

We all know about the unwritten law of keeping pregnancy on the down low until that fabled magically anointed 12th week. So many things can happen in those 12 weeks and we have been unknowingly stifling any support that could be given in these tiresome weeks and often stuff down the opportunity for sharing and healing if the dreaded worst does arise.

We encourage a hush around the most exciting happening in some women's lives. Then, we dedicate an entire month to awareness of the worst thing that could happen that most women go through alone and never share. So, here is my list of reasons you might just want to shout from the rooftops and revel in your joy. Right. Now.

1. The first trimester can be the most taxing and even terrifying. So much new is happening and even if you're a seasoned mom it can be

invaluable to have someone by your side through the tiring tumultuous ups and downs of those first 12 weeks.

2. What if you need some help? If it isn't your first rodeo and you've got little ones hanging from the curtain rods and swinging from light fixtures, having a village to run errands, fill your fridge, watch the tots while you put your still slim feet up, can be invaluable. Going these few months alone and in silence can be exhausting, especially if you're still trying to keep up with play dates and prior activity commitments.

3. You'll have a better excuse for your bloat than too many cookies. The first few months often bring more bloaty puffiness than glowy tightness of a goddess bump. It can be a bit more fun to show off that tumtum at the beach knowing that you don't need to try and hide or excuse it.

4. If you do have a history of loss, waiting out the first 12 weeks alone without so much as a whisper of your happiness and hopes, can be utter hell. Waiting, avoiding friends that may guess, pretending you love drinking water while everyone is enjoying wine...all the while you're bursting to share your secret for fear that you may not get to be happy for long. Not sharing the joy makes it even harder to share the torturous pain of a loss. Then, you're just alone. Alone with tears and fears and joy and pain and it's a horrible mixed up soup that could just be avoided by living in the moment. Be pregnant today, enjoy it, share it. What will happen tomorrow will happen tomorrow but has nothing to do with the joy of today and this moment. Live it for what it is. Now.

5. There are an average of 40 weeks of gestation for a human pregnancy. If a hush is in place for the first 12 weeks that is over a third of a full pregnancy that you don't get to share. One third of the time that the world sees you as a life giving human creating goddess, shushed and hidden. No reveling in the special treatment that pregnant women often enjoy. Nope. I say, take back that third of your time and share the joy.

6. If you share your news with your closest peeps first, you're more likely to be graciously excused when you yawn at 7pm or sleep in past 9am. If you aren't hiding your news you'll likely have people offer you amazing things like naps and chocolate.

7. Sharing makes it real. Sharing joyous news creates community and gives life to the hopes and dreams you have for that tiny embryo growing in your womb. Sharing and acknowledging this new person builds something that no silence ever could. Confidence, love, support, trust... a village.

So, whether you're holding an ultrasound photo of a yolk sac or leaning over the toilet in despair, I encourage you to share your journey and your deep love and joy for this new person that will change the world, your world, our world. We're all in this together.

I RAN OVER A PUPPY AND THIS IS WHAT I LEARNED

This isn't a piece about how I feel about nearly killing a small sweet animal. It's not about the impact of squishing a baby dog.

This is a piece about how much we don't realize our minds will react to external stimuli even when we think we know what's happening.

This is a piece about lies. It's about how I lied about running over a puppy and didn't even know it.

Last Friday when we left town our neighbors two border collie pups were at our house. We loaded up and headed out. Kind of. We could barely leave our house and getting down our long driveway was painful. I just knew I was going to squish one of them. They darted back and forth in front of the Yukon. Play bowing and wrestling. It took forever to get to the road. Maybe not forever but at least 10-15 minutes. I was so anxious.

When we arrived home on Sunday we had guests come in while we were putting the kids down. They expressed the same terror at nearly mangling the pups. The passenger even got out and walked with the pups to prevent them from being hit.

In my head I was already building a story of how it was going to be for me. What would end up happening and how it was just bound to happen and I would be the one. After all, I travel the driveway the most.

Later on Sunday, I was driving up the driveway when I saw the pups run up to my car. I was already going slowly but I slowed way down. Crept. The two of them were quite hard to keep track of on my own and I kept watching the mirrors and out the windows. So slow. Just creeping along. I was frustrated and starting to get nervous. It was going to happen and I had no idea how to prevent it. I honked. I honked some more and crept along.

Finally, in my side mirror I saw them both dart off toward their house. I saw them both clearly. And then, as I turned forward and thought about picking up speed, it happened. I heard yelping. I felt fear. There was no bump bump. No thump. No crushing squish. I just heard a baby pup in pain. It was instant. It was unexpected and I immediately reacted.

My brain took over. It took over everything. What my body did to stop the car. What my mind interpreted about what happened. My response of picking up the pup and walking it to the neighbors instead of driving there so the second pup didn't get hit. My brain just took over.

I knocked on the neighbor's door holding a trembling whimpering puppy. We're friendly with one another and they yelled to come in. I yelled back for them to come out. All I could think of was their two young daughters seeing their hurt pup. The husband opened the door and saw me with their pup and his face clouded over. Fear.

I explained what had happened. Well, I explained what I thought had happened. I hadn't ran the puppy over. I was sure of it because I hadn't felt anything bump. He must have been hit or spun by the tire. He must have ran right under the car. He had circled around. I tried to piece it together the best I could. I didn't know what happened, not really but I knew I hadn't ran him over.

I lied. I had no idea it was a lie. And here's how I came to the conclusion that it was actually a lie.

In the split seconds after the hit. My brain took over. It remembered my story that was built about this happening. It remembered how I said it would happen. It remembered what I had already created. This creation and the ingrained need to keep myself safe was what drove the story I told myself in those seconds after hearing the yelp. I didn't actually run over the pup. I couldn't have. I didn't feel a bump. There's no way I ran him over. I would never do such a thing. Never.

I helped look him over. I was in shock. Shaking. I kept repeating that I was sure he didn't actually get ran over. The truth is that I wasn't actually sure. You see, our minds are so wired to keep us safe that they will actually lie to us about memories. Even when something has just happened. It's fresh. And yet, we really don't know what happened.

How do I know that my story, the story that my brain told me and that I told my neighbor was a lie? Well, that little puppy went to the vet on Monday and as it turns out, he can't walk because he has a broken pelvis. A pelvis that was broken from being run over. I ran that pup over.

The honest to God truth is that I would never lie about that. But I did because I didn't know it was actually a manufactured observation of my own mind trying to keep me safe. Not from being wrong or being a bad guy but from the actual idea that I am capable of squishing an animal.

I am capable of running over a puppy. I know this because I ran over a puppy.

I made running over a puppy mean something about me in that split second and from there, my brain took over. Being the kind of person that would run over a puppy is the kind of person I imagine as careless, cold, even psychotic. My mind is uncomfortable with this meaning. Because admitting that I ran over a defenseless puppy dredges up a whole lot of other baggage and fears other than what really happened.

What happened?

I ran over a puppy that was running by my car.

That's it.

It doesn't mean anything about me. It doesn't define me. I'm not a puppy squisher or a psychopath. I am still a whole and complete human.

But, that wasn't the instant story that was spun up by my ever present meaning making mind.

It's not that I'm saying I'm a liar. It's not that I'm saying I lied and that's ok because my mind made it up. What I'm saying is that I trusted my mind and observational sensation to provide me with the truth. I really knew what happened was real and true. I believed that. I trusted my brain and it didn't give me the truth. It gave me what I wanted to be the truth.

The truth here is that we don't always know the truth. We don't know what happened. We don't even know what didn't happen. We only know our interpretation of the event. We only know a view. This is why we must, I stress MUST, always be open to what others have to say. It may really be a truth for them. We must always see others as a contribution to our lives. We must always accept that we are only the creators of our story and that we all have one.

I would never ever run over a puppy. Except, I did.

SAVORING

I watch his movements and the way his lashes flutter when he's just about to solve a mystery. I watch his dimpled fingers strain to do something new and challenging.

I will my brain to hold on. I command my memory to imprint these moments so I can recall them later. I struggle to crawl out of that space and just be.

Be with the learning. Be with the growing. Just be.

I want to hold on.

I also want to move with them, hold their hands as they grow, watch their eyes change color as the sights of the world impact who they'll be.

So, I snap a few pictures and set down the phone, I watch and laugh and let the moment pass. The sting of loss fades as the overflow of life and living and joy replace it.

The space of longing is cramped and small. The space of being and growing is so much more welcome.

Intention.

I catch myself sliding into sadness at the loss of the moments slipping away. Intention pulls me back.

There is no loss.

Just this.

Just right now.

And right now.

And right now.

And now.

This sweet moment is gone. But it's gone with joy and the next moments came and went as well.

It flows.

Holding on to the banks of the river only serves to drive my head under.

I'm learning. I'm learning from their savoring.

SOMETIMES

Sometimes, I experience myself as grumpy. I often forget that I'm just as responsible for that way of being as I am intentional powerful joy.

Sometimes, it takes acknowledging it to really get the impact.

"I'm being grumpy right now. I'm expressing frustration about this situation. I'm also hungry and having trouble keeping myself together while managing you guys. Mommy is having a meltdown."

Seeing the empathy on a child's face when you do the thing you're always telling them to do...It's humbling. It's also kinda scary.

But guess what, it is what it is and by owning my own shit they are learning to own theirs.

...Or that I'm an inconsistent crazy person.

Sometimes, I yell. Sometimes, I blame them for my upsets. And sometimes, I take responsibility.

I'm hoping my kids learn that we're not perfect and that's ok. I'm hoping that even if they blame others for their emotions sometimes, that taking ownership most of the time gives them power over it.

I have mom guilt and shame and all the other crap that seems to tag-along with the momming gig. I see their little faces look up at me when I'm losing my shit and grasping for peace.

They're always watching and learning. I'm teaching them something, even the times it's not what I want them to learn.

I'm learning that I'm the perfect example of imperfection and that's ok too.

Today, in Costco, I had an experience of myself as grumpy. I didn't snap, I didn't yell and I didn't do anything that needs apologizing for. But I get to say and I get to choose what happens next and that gives me power over the grumpiness...

Just as soon as I eat something and get these tiny humans down for a nap.

BREAKING POINT

Over the last couple weeks, I have pushed the person I have understood myself to be. I have pushed so hard that I can only imagine a breaking point is near. Except that it's not. The breaking point is a figment of my imagination and an end result that I've made up to keep me safe.

I have been headlong in the self-publishing world promoting and strategizing an assent for an incredible author and all the while the voice over in my head runs.

You're not good enough.
No one takes you seriously.
What do you think you're doing?
You have no idea how to do this.
You're little positivity act is going to crack soon, you will fail, you'll fall on your face and when you do, everyone will see it.

You think you can publish a book too? Silly girl, no one would read it. This is what success looks like; you're not a success.

You should quit now before you bring everyone else down with you.

So, as I set up accounts on sites I've always been terrified of, and as I scour the internet to learn everything I can about everything I need right now, and as I prod my resistant machine of a brain for new and fresh ideas, I sigh.

I sigh from exhaustion. I sigh from disgust. I sigh from elation. That voice may be running in a loop over every single thing I do but there are moments of pause. The moments when I conquer a mystery. The moments that I break through something that has always been a barrier. In those moments, the voice fades out; it chokes on its own fodder and as I basque in the momentary glory, I hear it whisper...

I was wrong.
You ARE extraordinary.
You can do it.
You are stronger than this voice.

Then, doubt. And the loop begins again. I've learned to ignore it. Dismiss it. I've learned through awareness and mindfulness to just hear it and not actually listen. I've learned that the only power that voice has is the power I give it by acting on its poison.

I've learned that I am enough, even if what I am today is less than yesterday, my best is subjective to the moment. I am enough. I can do anything. I do accomplish the impossible.

I am.
I can.
I do.

THE WASTING OF WAITING

I've been crying a lot lately. Not like, a few tears streaming down my face, we're talking the ugly cry. Blubbering. Snot dripping. Choking on a lump in my throat. It's the same struggle I've had for quite some time but it's recently gotten so intense that I am overwhelmed by waves and waves of emotion.

What am I doing with my life? Why do I care about anything other than this current moment? If today were my last day on earth how would my kids remember me? Am I giving myself to what I'm passionate about? Am I wasting my gifts out of fear or excuses? What the hell is the point of everything we do? Working? Earning money? All the stuff we surround ourselves with?

It's not one specific question that triggers me, but as I went through our morning in my head yesterday, I wondered if my son would remember the day he stopped biting people or if he'd just remember all the things his mother did to get him to stop. Soap in the mouth. Slapping of lips. Squeezing of cheeks. Yelling. Time out. Spanking. Hugging. Time in. More attention. Less attention. Ignoring. Biting back. Would he remember the lesson or the trauma? And, what was the point of it all.

We are here for such a short time. We only get this tiny window of that short time to be with our children and in that tiny space is this millisecond of each age and phase. Biting is one of those. What is the point in my practically beating it out of him when I know how stubborn he is and it's likely a phase. It will pass, just as the time that I have with him. The only thing that will remain for him is the experience of me not accepting him as perfect, whole and complete.

Why am I not writing. The excuses and reasons I have are completely invalid if compared to the amount of time I have to live and contribute to the legacy of humanity. But, I don't know how to monetize my blog or get published or...blah blah blah. It doesn't matter. None of it matters. I'm going to die some day. All those excuses will die right along with all the words I never wrote, all the experiences I never shared. The smiles and hugs I didn't give. All of it, gone.

All of it. All of the stuff, what is it for if not to avoid the intangible truth that it is all just bullshit. We are entirely responsible for creating our lives and moving through each experience with the integrity of the commitments we make.

At this point, looking in, I have been more committed to my reasons and excuses than to the actual living of life. Yes, there have been moments and stretches of clarity but it takes focus. The focus to look fear in the eyes and straight up tell it to take its reasons and excuses and fuck off.

Why do I care about my kid biting? Fear. What if he doesn't grow out of it? What will people think of him, of me.

Why do I not write? Fear. What if I don't get published, what if I never see my name in print; what if my writing is shit...what if I don't matter?

It's nothing. It means nothing.

I've been having this conversation with my husband, my sister, myself and although it brings me incredible sadness to think about how many of our precious moments are wasted doing whatever, it also brings me a feeling of being powerful. My life is mine because I say. I am awesome and brilliant and crazy fierce because I say so. I declare it.

All that runs through my mind as the tears stream in sheets down my cheeks. I'm choosing. I choose living. I choose action.

So, today I'm acting. I'm moving. Because time is like an escalator, it's going to take me to the end no matter how much I try and stay where I am or step backward.

I called occupational therapy to check on the referral for my sensory processing kid.

I measured my body parts and committed to getting healthy.

I'm writing one piece per day.

I set up emails to send memories to my kids.

I choose. I cry. I live.

FIGHTING MYSELF

Yesterday something happened that forever changed how I see and react to my strong willed, off the wall, sensitive and often impossible to deal with child. It changed how I will interact with all of my children.

I was downstairs and heard my three year old and two year old run up stairs to play in their room. I heard them stop on the stairs and then I heard my two year old daughter screaming. It was pain screams. Scared screams. I was already on my way around the corner to the stairs when I heard my three year old son run off and hide.

My little girl was crying alligator tears and trying to tell me that 'Wyatt did it' through sobs and choking on slobber.

I guess it freaked me out. Seeing her on the stairs with her hair all messed up and snot and slobber and tears running everywhere.

Knowing she could have been hurt badly by being pushed down the stairs. Her face triggered something in me and I snapped.

I ran as fast as an overweight pregnant woman in her third trimester can move. When I got to him he was already huddled on the floor terrified of my screaming his name. We don't spank but I do have a tendency to yell when I'm freaked out and he is so sensitive it just takes one bark to put him in tears.

He was crying. Sobbing.

I didn't take a moment. I didn't count to ten. I didn't breathe. I just thought of the story I had about him purposely hurting others just to get a reaction. I thought of his lack of empathy and his lack of caring when confronted with his actions. I saw him, this tiny huddled sobbing mess, as a threat to my other children, possibly even a threat to myself as a mother. I saw him as my failure and fear all rolled into this little rack of bones and spunk.

He looked up at me, terrified. My face must have been just horrible with all that boiling inside of me. I grabbed him by his fragile bony arms and stood him up on noodle legs. He faltered and I forcefully stood him up again.

By now he was blubbering. Snot and tears and sorrow gushed out of him. He looked pathetic. Not in the sense of someone you feel sorry for but pathetic like a beaten animal that has just given up. His spark, his weird quirkiness, gone. Just this tiny lanky lump of gut wrenching brokenness.

I looked at him for a millisecond before I began screaming,

"What did you do to her?! What did you do to her?! What did you do?!!!"

For a brief moment I was screaming at every single person that ever hurt me. I was screaming at my Step-dad, my mom, shithead bullies, my ex-husband...even my current husband. I was screaming at my past as I held the arms of this tiny precious boy that I grew in my womb and fed at my breast. I was hammering verbal fists on the chest of every vestige of pain and fear of being hurt or hurting others as my voice ripped through the heart of this vibrant perfect soul.

He gulped and tried valiantly to summon words.

He croaked,
"I don't know."

Like every other person I was screaming at, he didn't know what he did to hurt her. He did but he just couldn't articulate it. Or maybe he didn't because what he did didn't seem like it would cause pain.

As his tiny voice cut through the veil that hid his perfection, my heart fell. I heard that voice with my ears but felt it in my being.

As I imagined all the things I could have done differently, all the ways I could have made this a peaceful experience, all the ways I could have avoided feeling like a fuckup, I mustered,
"I think if you can take a breath and tell me what happened we can help Ellie feel better. I need to know how and where she got hurt."

In that quick change of voice, that moment, his mother was before him instead of some hateful monster, he changed. His slumped shoulders squared a little and his nose sniffed in and he wiped his tear streaked cheeks. He still stumbled through and gulped on the words but it was then that he could say what happened. In that suddenly safe space.

"I...I was... I was twying to hoewd her hands to get her to pway wif mmmme."

My. Heart. Broke.

A million pieces of myself were crushed by a forceful wave of mom guilt and then washed out into the foam of shame. Floating, bobbing, pieces of my promises to be a better mom, be the best version of me, not ruin my babies... The weight of the wave choked me and I grabbed his little rag doll body and pulled him in so tight I thought he might break.

"I'm so sorry. I'm so sorry. I'm so so so sorry."

As I sobbed into the orange hair on his tiny head he wrapped his spaghetti arms around me. I just felt it all. Every side-eye, snappy response, arm grab, less than loving retort I gave him. I felt my story of him as this hurtful soulless being...I felt it all, climbing my throat and threatening to choke the rest of what I could call life from my heart.

His now calm, articulate voice said,

"I'm sorry too mommy. I wanted to pway wif her but she didn't understand me. I'm sorry too."

At this time his sister came in and saw us hugging. She wrapped her arms around us and said she was sorry too. She apologized to her brother for screaming and not playing with him. He apologized for pulling her up the stairs by her hair and pulling on her hands. We hugged some more.

I followed them down stairs feeling defeated. Yet heartened at their love and empathy for each other. I sat in the living room in a daze. My heart actually hurt.

A few minutes later my three year old boy came in and said he was sorry again. I stopped him and said,

"Wyatt, I accept your apology and forgive you. I need you to know that

I'm sorry too. Screaming and scaring you was bad manners of me and I'm sorry. I know I hurt your feelings and scared you. I'm sorry. You are a kind and gentle boy and I love you. You have good manners."

He grabbed my hands and said,

"We both had bad manners mommy. I forgive you too. We just have to do better next time."

And just like that, it was done.

Will he remember that moment later when he hears my thundering footsteps? Will he think he is less than worthy and cower because he thinks he'll get screamed at? Will it be one of those things that lurks in the back of his development and manifests itself later in adult life?

Who knows. What I do know is that when I am angry with him I am actually angry at someone else that I don't have the balls to confront. Someone or something in my past.

That's the way of it. That's the cycle. That is how these things proliferate. Am I perfect? No. Absolutely not. Do I want to be? Not really.

What I hope for and strive for is knowledge. I hope to know why I feel triggered by my daughter's safety being challenged. I want to know why I feel triggered by the defiance in the face of a tiny person. Because, when I know why and where that ball of fury comes from I can confront it and move into a place of completion. A place of peace.

My son Wyatt has tested me today but in none of the interactions have I felt like he was less than love. The story I built about him was mine and he had no part in it. When I let that go I could clearly see how off it was.

I share this because I know there are mothers and fathers out there that fight their own stories and their own demons from the past. They fight them personified as their boss, co-worker, family member and even their children. I share this because describing my baby being yelled at by his mother may trigger in someone else the realization that they aren't alone and that that little person being yelled at is part of your heart and soul but has nothing to do with the past pain you want to hurl daggers at.

I share out of humility and healing.

HELLO DARKNESS

As a preface to the words that follow I'd like to say, I wrote this in the moments of descent. The plunging into something that I'm all too familiar with.

So many women suffer each day with postpartum depression and live in shame about it. So many women are patted on the head by loved ones and told, 'it's just hormones, you'll be fine.' The problem is, it's not fine, it won't be fine and women need to help each other. The day after I wrote this I called my psychiatrist of nearly 10 years and asked for the usual. Yes, I even used those words.

I didn't ask for help after my first child. I toughed it out because people closest to me patted my head. I don't fault them but in hindsight I think we all thought it was just a little baby blues and then it just wasn't. I lost the first six months of that child's life to darkness. I only have pictures of the perfection. I don't honestly have memories of those times that don't involve tears.

My second and third babies I was armed and ready. I had done enough reading to know what I was up against. I waited for the darkness to fall and then, made a call to my doctor. Within days I was new, fresh and happy. It doesn't work like that for some. I get that. I am fortunate.

I share this as an example of just how dreary and alone it can feel. I read it now and know the progression of it and that I sit here, well and together and sad for that woman. She is me but I am not her.

This is for all who suffer. I see you.

Hello Darkness, My Old Friend

Tomorrow will mark one week since I went into active labor. The wee hours of Friday will be a week since my youngest child was born. This is said to be a happy place. The glow and sparkle of that all too magical experience of birth, fading and the newborn smell ever under my nose... These are the golden hours. The days that will blur and fade and I'll strain to remember each detail, snapping as many pictures as I can just to hold on to the already slipping bits of reality.

The darkness descends. It comes down and fills up and closes in. This sinking feeling in my heart pleads for anyone, someone to save me. Throw me a rope, a life ring, give me their hand. But, it wouldn't matter. I felt it coming. I saw the first signs yesterday and woke in the night to the fear that I would lose myself to it once again. As I stayed in my bed, motionless, aware of the ache in my pelvis where only days ago a child dwelled, aware of the adult diaper filling with blood and tissue that cradled a life, aware of my heart pounding to pump life around my flabby body, I felt hot tears streaming down my face.

I honestly had hoped to escape it. To pretend I could smile my way through it this time. I hoped I could get one baby, one precious baby that would save me from the blackness that steals my sunny joy and replaces it with sticky guilt and lingering doubt. I ran. In my mind at least. I thought that reading more about it or being pro-awareness would earn me points. Instead, I'm about a week and a half ahead of schedule.

Tears. I don't know where they come from or how I haven't run out already and it's only been a little over a day. The feared quicksand of childhood has crept into this adult moment and is already crushing my chest. Only no one can see and I'm grasping for sticks and grass and hands. So many hands. So many people that would offer a hand if only a hand would do anything to pull me out.

I wasn't going to share. I wasn't going to write. I had planned to go it in silence this time and share my weight loss and eating journey instead. But, I sit here, tears still streaming and deadlines for other projects I've already been paid to write, piling up, and I'm thinking, fuck it. Other people suffer. Other women choke in the sand pits and their hands just freeze there, eventually lifeless and empty, waiting for someone to grasp it, if only for a little warmth.

I see you.

I may be hunkered down in my hole of wretched stinking life sucking postpartum depression but I still see you and I know that when you text your friend that you're sad, you really mean you feel like your heart is dying. I see you.

I know that when you cry and they say, 'it's ok, it'll get better.' you want to believe them but you can't even believe you'll take your next breath. I see you.

I know that when you hear, 'just be positive,' inside you want to punch those words in the face because you are deep enough in it that positive doesn't even look the same anymore. I see you.

I also see you, knowing that all of these feelings are just feelings. I see you fighting with everything in your power to not make it mean anything about you and to just let it be what it is. I see you not wanting to give it power or control, just rolling with it, knowing there is an end, even if you can't see it yet. I see that too because I'm there with you.

THE HIGH CHAIR

I found myself just staring, willing it to have a purpose, hoping it would have one more chance to be needed. I knew those thoughts were ridiculous. There would not be a need for it in our home, except maybe for guests.

The high chair.

Ellie had abandoned it over a month ago but I just couldn't do anything about it. At the moment there are several extra chairs just milling around the dining room anyway so it wasn't completely out of place. I stood there in my quiet house and looked at that high chair. Grubby crusted seat cover. Marked and scuffed plastic. I have no idea where the tray, with all it's cut marks and scratches, is.

I just stood there.

Staring.

Yes, this is a bit dramatic but I'm trying to 'be' with my emotions lately and as it turns out this method seems to be helping my 'bottle it up' tendencies. So, there I was, staring at this filthy chair. Little Ellie was down for a nap and the boys were off terrorizing the neighbor. I moved it to the rug, like I always do, and then swept up a week's worth of crumbs. As I went to move it back to the middle of the dining room a wave of nostalgia washed over me. I thought of the first time I put Hank in that chair. How I propped him up with towels and fed him mushy avocados and applesauce. He was too little to be in that chair but he was so advanced and amazing for his age, as all first children are, we rushed him into everything before he was ready. I thought of little red headed Wy, poking blueberries around the tray and then tasting them. Watching his pudgy fingers shove berries into his face as fast as an uncoordinated baby can...Then Ellie, her precise pincer grasp and her tidy munching. She left the chair earlier than the boys. I think she got tired of feeling left out.

The baby swing is long gone. The jumperoo and the baby papasan seat. Numerous toys and gadgets, gone. The high chair is still here and so is the crib. We still need them. Well, until this last month... Now, just the crib stands between my baby and having no babies at all. There's something really sad about that to me. It's the end of an era. I've heard a lot of women say that they just knew when they were done having babies. A switch went off in their heads and they dropped their husbands off at the urologists office without flinching. For me, I don't think I am equipped with that switch. The decision was more or less made and I relented because there's no fighting or winning when making people is involved. So, I put it away. The dream of more babies. I folded it up and tucked it away, just as I did with the high chair today.

I turned my back and walked away and my heart felt heavy. It's a high chair. A. High. Chair. So, yeah, there's obviously more brewing under the surface.

The thing I can't seem to unwrap is that I don't even know if I'd really want to have another baby. The idea of not having another one slashes my heart. I love the babies I have. I am satisfied that I have done my part to populate the world with intelligent attractive people (go on, hate if you want, every mom knows their babies are just the best). Do I really need to have more? Do I really need to tempt fate and risk an unhealthy baby or a complicated pregnancy? Am I just in love with the idea of that stage of life so much that I'd torture myself by going back or worse, questioning if I really even want to?

There are teeny tiny baby clothes stashed everywhere. In the garage. Under our bed. Crammed in closets. I can't bring myself to get rid of them and I really don't know why. I don't believe there are more babies in my future but I just can't let go. The high chair is folded up in the mudroom. I will walk by it daily. Really, I may have passed sanity on this one and jumped head long into delusional. When my husband says he doesn't want any more babies I burst into tears. Yet, if he were to say, he doesn't care either way, I should decide, I have no idea what I'd choose. I really don't. That's the part that makes me sad. I'm indecisive on something as monumental as creating an entire human being and then being responsible for nurturing it into a productive member of society.

If only it were as simple as a high chair.

HELL FOUND ME

Hell found me. I had anticipated it's approach. The leering stares from behind corners and out of crevices. I had smelt it's putrid breath on the warm summer breeze. It lurked in the wee hour darkness of night and climbed around my fretful dreams in the precious few hours of sleep.

Hell found me, and as prepared as I thought myself to be, it crashed into me and the gurgle of my drowning soul was heard by no one. I reached out and gasped for breath, flailing for a hand to pull me to safety, freedom.

Hell found me, in the late night of my new baby's fourth week of life outside my warm and nurturing womb. It descended upon me while I looked into my sweet tiny son's sleepy eyes. I looked down at him, his mouth full of my chapped and bleeding nipple, and the dam of tears destroyed any attempt of composure as it burst and mocked my control.

Hell found me, held me, and tormented me for nine months as I choked on my own pleas for help. I sobbed in the bathroom, alone in the mornings, before my husband could see my agonizingly fake smile. It strangled the words, I rehearsed, to request the help I knew I needed.

Hell found me, filled me with shame, blame and a horrific fear, that someone would see it, clinging to my back, and take my precious baby away. It stole the joy from those early memories and erased so many sweet smiles and babbling coos from my treasury of mothering gems. It left me blank and weary, constantly shifting and itching for something I feared would never be mine.

Hell found me...my soul knew it was all a facade. I was faking a life of smiling. My being knew it was all lies I told myself that I could make it go away, at any moment, if I chose to scream louder, reach farther, be seen. My heart threatened to quit, just stop it's beating, pled for me to do something, anything, to pull free of hell's poisonous barbs.

Hell may have found me but it eventually got bored and moved on. The infection and festering moved through its process of healing and left a bright red scar across that time of my life. I woke up one morning and felt lighter, decongested, free.

Hell found me, when I had my next baby, but this time, I was ready.

MISCARRIAGE

One in five women will have a miscarriage. Does it make it any easier? No. It also doesn't seem to make the general population any more sensitive or sympathetic. Things like, "Thankfully you weren't that far along." Or another good one, "Everything happens for a reason." Are not usually what a grieving hormonal woman wants to hear. No matter how far into the pregnancy that loss occurs it can be devastating.

I, for instance, had two miscarriages prior to conceiving and carrying my three children. I was young, he was young and well, we weren't married, weren't very stable and we definitely weren't ready. I still think of those lost babies. I think, I could have a seven year old (they were back to back by a couple months); she'd be this or he'd be that. I wonder if they would have had my eyes (all three of my little one's have their dad's eyes) or if she would have had my hair. I wonder about his personality and if he would be much different than our two little boys. When the due date rolls around I imagine them celebrating their birthday and how big they'd be getting. Yes, this may seem slightly morbid but it's how my mind works and I know I'm not alone.

Miscarriage isn't something that gets talked about. There are no sympathy cards... "I'm so sorry your baby wasn't viable and nature spared you the agony of childbirth." Uh, no, there's no card or easy comfort to give. For the most part I feel like women suffer mostly alone. Their families try and be strong for them or ignore it so they themselves don't have to grieve too. It's a sad lonely thing but we're not alone.

Losing a baby is never easy. It's not easy when you know it was barely a plankton, looked like a seahorse or almost had a heart beat. It's not easy when you've seen a heartbeat and then it wasn't there the next time. I can't fathom the loss of a breathing child but I know the loss of a child that mostly existed only in our minds, well, it's pretty agonizing. Sometimes we don't even want the baby that we lost and it's still sad.

My husband (the same man that fathered my two lost babies...yes, we matured and got our acts together) and I had mutually decided that our three perfect children were enough. When our daughter was born 6 1/2 months ago we had completed our family. I wasn't completely on board as I had always planned on popping babies out until my parts gave up or fell out.

As my daughter slowed down on breastfeeding, my cycle returned. I had one cycle and then this last one was expected 26-28 days later. It was late. First I didn't think anything of it. Then I was tired, my boobs hurt a bit, I was nauseated in the evenings and lightheaded throughout the day. By day 4 I asked my husband to buy me a home pregnancy test. He said he'd like to wait it out. On day 6 I woke up, sat on the toilet and thought, "This is it, I'm pregnant. I will now be unable to pack my kids into shopping carts and...oh, the car, how am I gonna get them all in the car and..." I know these are pretty selfish and random thoughts but, I had just woke up and had also just come to terms with being a mother of three.

Previously, when I had known I was pregnant, even before I tested, I was loopy with anticipation and joy. I couldn't wait to pee on a stick and know that a line would appear. This time was different. We hadn't tried to make this baby. We hadn't wanted to make a baby. We didn't want a baby. As I sat there, my feet going numb, I just started to wake up and get over the shock. I decided to go into town and buy a test. I thought about how I'd juggle my three kids and go to doctors appointments. I hoped it would be a girl. I started to feel a flutter of hope and happiness and excitement. Hey, we didn't plan it but babies are a blessing and we would be four times blessed. My husband was in the shower and I thought about his reaction. I knew he would hide his shock and show only happiness and support. I knew he'd never utter another word about only having three. He would love this baby like the three that we planned...and so would I. The range of emotions, from low to high, had me almost dizzy. I was pregnant...and I was happy.

As I planned my day I figured I'd give myself one more wipe since I forgot if I had peed again after my initial sleepy pee. Out of habit, I looked at the paper before dropping it in the bowl. Pink. There was a slight pink tinge on the paper. My heart sank. Crushed. The baby I didn't want wouldn't be. Another wipe confirmed that I was bleeding. No need to be worried or excited or happy...unless I was happy that I wasn't pregnant. Yes, I should have been happy. Elated. That's what I would do, be happy. I had dodged a bullet.

I left the bathroom and put on my happy face. I told my husband that my period had arrived and we could both stop stressing. And then, something strange, I felt intense relief. Like, I just kept breathing deep and saying, "Phew, thank God!" It was surreal. My heart was holding back sadness and my head was jumping for joy. This was a Thursday.

By Saturday I was on the phone with the on-call doctor explaining symptoms and worried that I was going to bleed to death. She told me I wouldn't bleed to death and that if I thought it was a 'chemical pregnancy' I should do a home pregnancy test and if it turned out to be positive I'd need to be seen in a month to check my hormone levels. I thought of my attitude while setting my appointment, just a week before, to discuss getting an IUD. I didn't want to accidentally get pregnant. Did I?

Sunday sucked as I just knew I was losing an embryo that could have been my blonde haired princess or the annoying little brother... Monday I finally broke down and bought a test. Yep, two blue lines. Two lines. I was losing a baby not a blob or a chemical or a blighted ovum, it was a baby, my baby and it was gone. Seeing the positive test really sent me over the edge. Up until the positive test it was just the imagination of a sleep deprived mother. Nope, that baby I didn't want had left or was leaving my body. I cried.

When I told my husband he softly replied that he already knew. He said he just didn't want to admit it or acknowledge it. I told my best friend and my sister. The rest of the world...no one knew about my bittersweet two lines or the baby I imagined would make my life more difficult and yet so much sweeter. No one suspected my heart was weeping as I continued to post cute photos of my little ones on Facebook and write about my garden and digging in the dirt. No one knew about the struggle of wanting something that I thought I didn't want.

One in five women will miscarry. So many women yet such a lonely occurrence. For all you mamas of lost babies and for the poor daddy's that comfort their women while they wrestle with their own grief and cocktail of emotions... You are not alone. Just knowing that helps me breathe. It helps me smile when I think of her blonde hair blowing in the breeze or the fire that would have danced in her eyes. It makes my heart hurt just a little bit less and that's enough to help the pain get a little more numb.

LET'S TALK ABOUT MARITAL DISCORD

As I pulled pieces of writing to compile and contribute to this book I stumbled upon one that took my breath away. It was oozing with pain and dripping with everything I'd ever feared about intimacy.

The piece that follows this is a stark reminder that I am never fully present to what could be next, what a blessing pain and sorrow can be and what can be build from what seems like the ashes of ruin.

When I read it again, my gut tightens. I remember the moments but can't recall the trigger. Nothing about the words feel real to me anymore but in the moment they were so real. The feelings and emotions, the fear and longing, it was all real.

Had I unplugged myself from that outlet of life, things would have been so different. I'd never have learning that my husband has a story about needing to make me happy and having me feel important. I never would have learned that he gets triggered when I act like I'm not important to him. He goes off the ledge because what I'm implying is so far from what he's committed to that he can barely contain his failure story about himself.

In times of abject trauma there is something to glean.

I'm thankful each day that I have my husband in my life as a partner in our journey. It could have been so much different and because of that, I've chosen to include the pain of the pit that I once found myself in.

PAIN AS OBSERVED

I don't know how to explain what happened. I guess I'll stumble through it and possibly make some sense of it along the way. Maybe.

I was standing there, feeling unheard and unseen but naked and vulnerable just the same. I was standing there feeling unimportant and pushed aside. I was standing there wondering what my monetary worth would actually be. If someone were to purchase me, how much would they pay? What is it actually worth to own someone and own the say in their life? I was standing there with all this churning inside of me while trying to listen to him and not erupt in a childish, "This is not fair!" rant and trying desperately to see what he was saying through his clenched teeth and tight fists. I was trying. But, as Yoda said, there is no try, only do. I failed at hearing his voice roar in my ears. I failed at seeing his viciousness coil for the strike. I failed at holding myself together. I failed at being strong for my children. There was no winner but so much failure.

I stood there and heard my voice weaken. I heard my whimpering voice plead for him not to yell. Please don't yell in front of the kids. Please don't do this, please don't yell. Please. Please. I could hear my voice crack, my chin drop shaking, and my heart, I felt it dry and shrink from him. What little there was left in there, whatever was left of the full bloom of our love, I saw it wither, petals scattered by the force of his fury, and crumble under the weight of all the promises dropped on top, forgotten. I felt myself becoming a child. A terrified little girl, clinging to the promise of a new day. I felt her shudder and convulse. I felt her pulling me back, tucking me into safety.

Tears streamed down my cheeks and I began to act like an animal. I don't know what words I made, just sounds, whimpering and pleading. I shrunk then, as a person, no longer the strong competent willful woman, just a beaten down tortured child. A whimpering weakling begging for it to be over, wishing for a hole to crawl into. It didn't stop. I saw in his eyes a desire to strike me. Not physically but I could see that he saw my weakness, my tears and choked speech betrayed me. My slumped shoulders and cowering stance gave me away. He slashed and jabbed with words. The hits slammed hard on my raw heart. The trust I committed to building, the vulnerability I had spent months cultivating and encouraging in myself, blood splatter on the walls. Intricate droplets bursting forth from my soul as I struggled not to crumple to the floor. My daughter wailed and looked up at us. Blood spattered cheeks with the bluest blue eyes, her tears mixing with the blood of my wounded heart.

Then, somehow, I escaped. I walked out to go to the doctor to see if I could get help for the horrid sinus congestion I'd been enduring. This was what had started the fire. My request for time for myself. As I hitched in breath after breath and hunched at my steering wheel, unable to see out of my tear filled eyes, I saw his face as I walked away. It was clear as the screen I'm looking at now. It wasn't remorse I saw there,

there was no trace of that. No, it was something more frightening than the yelling and berating. More tragic than our children seeing me be verbally beaten to a bloody whimpering pulp. What I saw killed the last of what was once so important to me. What I saw was indifference. His face was hollow and spilling all the hate he had for the world. All the shitty clients and financial woes, the stress of having stress. His eyes didn't even see me. His bleeding, wounded wife.

I don't know how to explain what actually happened. I only know how it felt. I only know what was there before and what is gone now. I only know the sour aching feeling in my gut and the burning sting in my puffy eyes. I only know that I never want to feel that again. Ever.

ON THE LAST BABY

I've tussled with having another baby, after each baby. My husband and I struggled to get pregnant with our first live born baby and I feel a bit like a collector of sorts. Like I experienced scarcity in the beginning and now, I don't want the abundance to end.

Before writing this piece, I just knew we were done having babies and it tore at the fabric that I had woven in the story of what our life would look like.

Shortly after writing this piece, I got pregnant and subsequently lost that baby. That gave so much more weight to this longing.

Why Have Another Baby

My husband and I had always planned on having a large family. It the beginning of that journey we were told that we may never even have a single child. So, we charted and graphed and I peed on sticks and used a cycle tracker and we ended up having three amazing little ones with relatively little effort (let's not make this a birds and bees talk).

When our daughter, was born, my husband stared into her colostrum drunk eyes and declared that he felt complete. He felt our family was complete. She, my sweet and stubborn diva of a daughter, was our missing piece. I looked at him, looking at her, and in the flood of all that emotional postpartum soup, I heaved a sigh. It was heavy. Yes, I actually heaved it. I hoped that he was just feeling the instant love that you do when your sticky little spawn is placed in your arms. I was hoping that he'd come back around to our dream of a family of 6 or even more. Even as my lady bits were being soothed by an ice pack diaper my heart was longing to do it all again. I needed just one more.

Now, here we are. Our little girl is now 15 months old. My heart aches to write that. The age span between our first and second child is 20 months and the span from two to three is 15 months. Our little one is now the age that her brother was when she arrived.

My uterus is very empty. She is also past the age that her next sibling would be much less than 2 years younger than her. We had planned on having our babies pretty close together and as she grows and wears her brothers clothes I actually feel phantom babies in my uterus.

Anyhow, I have reopened the topic with my husband; although my biological clock has plenty of time left on it our plan of how our family would be doesn't allow for dilly dally. Unfortunately, I think this dream of mine, may just have to be let go. My husband has not changed his mind. Not even a little bit. As I watch him soothe his little girl at night, like only he can, I wonder if I'm truly being selfish. Why do I need another baby. I have three amazing people in my life that were grown in my body and then pushed out into the world without much trouble. I am deeply blessed. So, why. Well, I answer this with an abstract...

Dear Fourth Baby, Second Daughter, Blessing,

My sweet delicate daughter that won't be... I can see you now, just getting your legs under you, standing in the prickle of freshly cut grass. Your bright golden hair glints in the sun and glimmers of tangerine shine like a halo atop your sweet head. You turn to me, with a bounce and a giggle, and your bright blueberry eyes dance and sing in the shadow cast by your face. The skin of your nose is pink and I can see freckles in your future. Your daddy's freckles. Freckles like your aunties. Freckles like your ginger haired brother. The lips below your pink button nose are full as a summer peach and nearly the same color. I can barely see them for the laughter that pours out is all consuming. You look to me and then your big sister as we try to show you a dance. Your round tummy shakes as you giggle all the way to your tiny nubby toes. Big sister takes your hand and tries to spin you around. You both fall to the green spiky grass as two superhero boys come running through your path. As you stand and right your dirty rumpled hand-me-down dress your arms stretch toward me. You reach for me, your imaginary mama, for a hug that I'll never give.

Very truly yours,

Your longing mama

PART **5**

ODES AND NOTES

"Be the freshness in the face of stagnation of those that would shun what they don't understand. Tumble in the sea of creative query, never knowing what you are looking for but enjoying the tug of the energy that pulls you hither and yon."

ODE TO THE WANDERERS

Ode to my mother and every other wandering spirit that comes and goes. Be free, I love you.

Some souls wander, constantly seeking, searching, blowing and rolling in the winds of change. Some root deeply where they land and act as sturdy sentinels for their families. In a society of success driven money identity, and the longing to find our place, it is often feared to be a wild sort. It is made wrong by those that have no will to understand it nor compassion to see its beauty; shame overcomes the burnish and smooth edges of that tumbled gem.

I say, roll on. See and experience -- lay your weary heart open to the world. Share your dreams and the wilds that you've taken in. Be the freshness in the face of stagnation of those that would shun what they don't understand. Tumble in the sea of creative query, never knowing what you are looking for but enjoying the tug of the energy that pulls you hither and yon.

When you smile up at the sun, it is also my sun and when you count the stars, I too see them sparkle. I am the tree, you are the leaf...blow, blow away on that brisk wind. We are part of the same journey.

BECAUSE I SAID SO: AN ODE TO MY CHILDREN

I will not be the motivating mom.

I don't believe in motivation or divine cosmic bullshit. I don't believe it will ever be easier or harder or I'm ever going to feel like it. You probably won't either. That's ok. Do it anyway.

I don't believe in can't or should. These are traps that speak in your head to hold you apart from your greatness. Notice them but don't give them power. Hear them in your head right before you're about to do the impossible... then tell those words to back the heck off and watch this.

I do believe in momentum. In being and acting in direct correlation with a commitment to an outcome or effect. I believe in setting life in motion and building that snow ball until it's unstoppable – until you couldn't go back the other way if you wanted to. Believe me, you don't.

I think subtleties are for boutique fashion and bold out-there personality is for the thought shifter, the time bender, the world changer. I'll never stop you from being weird or different or dressing like a ninja princess knight with wings. I'll hand you a sword.

I believe that when someone tells you you're going to be a shitty X or a mediocre Y, that's your cue to blow life out of the water. Smash expectation to bits – lean so far into your action that you forget the critics and only remember the impact you're out to make. Be who you are and show up in all your greatness. I'll be right there to embarrass you with my sweary awkward cheering.

Being a world changer isn't hard. It's not easy either. Hard and easy are also words veiled with good intentions. Be mindful of those two. World changing is a shift in being. A shift so great that you won't be able to use the word mediocre. It's a stand for your own greatness and in knowing, with that single action, your greatness will shift the consciousness others. You will reach into souls and pull their awesomeness out into the open; it will kick and scream and hide – and you will hold it up to their eyes and watch as they see their own light. I'll do this to you over and over if I have to so you get the hang of it. After all, I've endured enough of your screaming to be immune to it for a good cause.

When the naysayers hold up their yield signs, you will look higher, farther and be blind and deaf to their calls and halts.
Push past opinions.
Push past circumstance.
Push until your soul wants to rip itself out of the body that can barely keep up.
And then, push a little more. Like I did to bring you into this world.

I recently learned that the probability of being you, of being me and of being a lone human in this world is 1 in 400 trillion. It's a cosmic joke. Every one of us is extraordinary just by virtue of being born. You are an effing miracle.

A miracle.

Never accept yourself as less that a miraculous happening. Never roll over and accept a fate you didn't create. Never accept less than your greatness.
Average, mediocre, plain... those aren't what you are.

Not ever.

If you ever doubt it, hear my voice telling you with unequivocal proof...

You are a miracle...

Because, I said so.

ON THE LOSS OF A DOG

When you have a great dog it's not something you need to think about to know; its something you can sense and feel in your being. Deep in your soul there's that gentle tug that pulls you to be with that furry beast and to love it and give it the opportunity to do what dogs do best, make us happy.

When you have a great dog you can feel it in your cheeks when you smile at their giddy face, flapping in the wind, of an open car window. When you have a really really great dog you can smell it in the scent of pure dog joy that comes from a magical spot near their velvety soft ears. You can hear it in their late night snore and feel it in breath on your face, from the chin on the bed, that wakes you up at 5am when it's just got to be time to go outside for adventure. A great dog, a really special dog will let you know it with the raise of their eyebrows when you say "ball" or the cock of their head when you whisper their name.

A great dog will push you to be your best. It will reveal in you an endurance that you never knew you possessed. A great dog will somehow get you to do the things you don't want to and help you to enjoy it. A great dog will ease your deepest agony, lick your tears and show you how to be strong, man up and move on. When you have a great dog you have a coach, a friend, a motivator, a sponsor... An angel by your side. This dog will hold you closer than any human could and never have to embrace you to do it.

When you have a great dog it's not easy to let it go. It's not easy to admit that you got more from a beast than you were ever able to give. When you have a great dog, no matter how many balls you've thrown, treats you've given, tummy scratches you've done... You will feel empty and broken that you didn't give more. You will feel torn open when you look into their eyes during your last goodbye. You will feel your guts turn and your heart split as their life slips from their vibrant trusting eyes. You will melt and turn to stone all at once. You will feel a piece of your heart tear free as you put their lifeless body to rest. This pain, this utter gruesomeness of emotion, this is a true sign, a real indicator, the best way to know that you, you were truly and undeservingly blessed with a damn great dog.

We love you Buddy. We always will.

THINGS I'VE LEARNED FROM MY DAUGHTER

I just celebrated my 31st birthday last month. It was relatively uneventful. 30 was far more momentous and even tragic for me. This, adding a one, a total breeze. During my birthday week, and that whole month really, I like to reflect back on my year and set new goals and really give myself the opportunity for a successful year. This year I was surprised by just how much of my reflection involved things I had gleaned from my adventures in mothering a little girl. Little girls are special. Not because they're especially different from little boys but because they are extraordinary, fierce, sweet and magical.

Of course there are far more than 10 things to learn and appreciate about having a daughter and in particular, my daughter, but who has all day to read lists.

1. Never let what you're wearing have a bearing on how much enjoyment you get out of a situation. So often I have stressed about what I'm going to wear or how I'm going to dress or look for an occasion. This was especially so before I lost almost 80 pounds last year. I had really lost the spark of enjoyment in being due to how I felt I looked in my clothing. My daughter never cares. Someday she may but I hope to prolong that as long as possible.

2. Never let an obstacle in your way prevent you from enjoying the adventure. Better yet, climb it and stand on top of it in awe of yourself. Enjoy the view and then move along.

3. Girls can do anything that boys can do but we don't have to or need to. It's okay to be a girl and not be even remotely apologetic about it. I love pedicures, getting my hair did, shopping and girl talk. I take joy in conquering laundry mountain. I find happiness in a freshly cleaned and organized pantry. I revel in craft time and like to bake. I'm sure I personify many other stay-at-home-mom cliches and, hey, I'm okay with that. My daughter never feels bad for having tea parties or playing dress up, why should I.

4. Hair schmair. It's just hair. My daughter happens to have copious amounts of hair for her age but she never really fusses about it. She sits still for a comb and a pony or barrette but not much more. She could care less what her hair looks like. I have adopted this ideal and now sport hair nearly as short as my husband. It doesn't make me any less of a person, less beautiful, or less feminine. It's hair.

5. It's ok to want to be held. It's ok to be picky about who holds you and it's ok to linger longer than you thought was appropriate. My little girl doesn't much care to snuggle me. There was a time after she weaned from breastfeeding that she still needed my snuggles. But, then one day it was like a switch turned off and she became a daddy's girl through and through. I've been the sole night waker up until her. It's been a few months now that she just must have her daddy rub her back so she can

sleep. I try but she just screams in my face and violently throws herself against the bars of her baby jail. Some nights I could just throat punch my smug husband as he returns from her room, victorious. She knows what she wants and makes no reasons or excuses. If I take it personally that's my deal.

6. Food is for eating. That's it. She doesn't seem to take much pleasure in food but doesn't dislike it either. When she's hungry, she eats. When she's not, food gets tossed on the floor. It doesn't matter how tasty or pretty or seasonal the food is; if she's not hungry, it just doesn't matter. I've spent my entire post pubescent life worrying about my weight, thinking about food, thinking about not thinking about food… it's exhausting to reflect on something so trivial having that much power in my life. It really is just food though. I still struggle with that but grow stronger in my convictions every day that I make better choices.

7. Mommy's are awesome, especially her mommy. I have a hard time with this one. My deep inner fear of not being good enough for my children has been debilitating on some days. Yet, my babies love me. They look at me with awe and wonder. They tell me they love me and they speak of me like I'm a goddess. My daughter, she doesn't really talk yet so her actions are all I have. I know she thinks I'm the greatest person on the planet by how she runs to hug me or the twinkle in her blueberry eyes when she smiles at me. To her, I'm the greatest mom that ever was or is. That is something that humbles my heart on the days I think I'm not enough.

8. Upset, meltdowns and fits are part of life. You should have your tizzy and then move along. Don't sit there and dwell on it and stew and roll around in it. Have the ugly cry and get over it. My sweet little diva is the best fit thrower I know. But, when it's done, it's done. She doesn't expect to be treated differently because she got upset. She just moves right along to the next thing. No worries. No apologies. Just expressed emotions and then she's done. If I only had half the courage and self awareness that she seems to have. I know in reality it's more of an

underdeveloped brain synapse situation but who's splitting hairs here. I'm inspired.

9. It is what it is. This is always present for me but I'm often reminded of just how powerful this little gem can actually be. I didn't learn this from her but I am reminded of it when I look at her. My daughter is my daughter. That seems redundant but bear with me. She is neither my last child, my only daughter nor my first daughter. I don't know what the future holds and imagining how it could be, would be or should be robs me of who she really is. My little girl is my little girl. Yes, she very well may be my first, last and only daughter. She may be the last baby I ever have. All the things I witness daily may be the last time I see it. It is what it is. Today is today and she is who she is as I am me. That is all. The rest is just a story that hides the preciousness of the now. The happening. The real and tangible moment.

And...

10. Girls are fun. They are different than boys and that's awesome. Girls think different. Girls act different. It's special and magical and causes me to actually drop my jaw daily. It really gives me pause and appreciation for all the things that make me different than my husband. It makes me thankful that I'm me. It makes me thankful for my daughter and that I was blessed with both genders of children so I can really appreciate that we are different and that's seriously fabulous.

DEAR BABYBEAR,

Numbered are the days that your tiny feet are more round than arched and your curious fingers spend infinitum poking at a bubble, as if the world depended on your insight and discovery. It does, little one, it does. Take your time small scientist. Be in the space of time, exactly how you experience it; let it flow around you, a tiny pebble in a free and wild stream. Just be.

SWEET SIX MONTH OLD, BABYBEAR,

I can't believe you're six months old! I've forgotten what it felt like to have you wriggle in my tummy. I've nearly lost the way you smelled when you were so fresh and sticky, the way you tried desperately to hold my gaze as you greedily nursed to sleep.

The days of teeny tiny clothes and quiet grunting coos are gone. You're getting so big every day. Your legs and arms are so big and strong and you have such drive and focus. Nary a green bean can escape your grasp. Your sweet joyous heart brightens our days and I honestly can't remember our life without you in it. You were our missing piece.

You completed our family.

Watching you navigate the crumbs and toys and siblings on the floor brings me pause. Were all my babies once this small and curious? Seeing you take pride in chewing a pickle or gnawing on a monster truck sends the blood rushing to my cheeks.

This is it.

Though all of the amazing things you're learning and doing are your firsts, they are my lasts. So, please don't make it mean anything about you if your pterodactyl squawk and steam rolling around the room is met with enthusiastic tears.

I'm savoring you.

I'm remembering your bothers and sister. I'm saying goodbye to so much but welcoming a limitless future. You're six months old now but soon you'll know it all and when you take your first steps in a few short months, please know that the tears that blur my sight will be joy leaking out of my soul.

You are perfect.
You are joyous.

You are strong and you are loved.

~Mom

DEAR WRIGGLING UNBORN,

As I lie here awake before the sun, and feel you moving inside your liquid universe, I feel hope. I hope that someday you will know how very much I've loved you from the start. From the first time I saw your tiny heart flicker on the ultrasound screen and you were nothing more than a tiny embryo holding onto your fragile yolk sac. Now you have grown into a delicate miniature of the baby I will meet in just a matter of months.

I am not surprised that I feel this tethered consciousness with you. I am by nature a very spirit driven, connection based, person. But as you roll and stretch my heart fills and can not contain this admiration I have for you. You've come so far. We have yet to meet but I feel as though I've known you many lifetimes.

I love you. I feel as though I've spent my life waiting to meet you. Like you are an angel and when our eyes meet my heart with burst and I will recognize you from all the times my spirit brushed yours and you pulled at that tethered awareness to remind me that we've already met.

My heart aches for the pains life will cause you. For the girls that will trample your precious heart. For the loved ones you will lose. For the disappointments and fears you will face. But My son, I love you, and you will never suffer alone. As you are with me now, connected in body by a tether of flesh, so will I be with you always by a tendril of awareness and love.

You have quieted down now. I feel you settling back into your world. Soon I will hold you and my voice will soothe you but for now we have our thoughts and no words need be exchanged.

THINGS PEOPLE SAY THAT COULD BE REPLACED BY A HUG

People mindlessly say things all the time. They find themselves in social situations and without really thinking it through they allow words to fall out of their overworked mouths.

This is especially true in talking to women with kids. I don't know why but we are approachable and must seem like we are receptive to all opinions regarding our kids, choices and even appearance.

Here are 5 comments that happen quite often that I wish would just be replaced with a hug.

1. You look great. You've held up great for having three kids.

Uh, thanks, I think... So, what does that really mean? I'm hot for a mom? I'm in a special category of attractiveness for the stretched out uterus sect? You think the fact that I have kids should have lessened my looks?

Here's the thing. I'm hot. I'm not full of myself. I'm smokin' hot because I had three kids and I have the confidence to think my mom butt looks incredible squeezed into high waisted skinnies. I grew three people inside my body in less than 5 years and I gained and lost over 150 pounds in the process, and obscenely enough, built so much confidence that it makes me sparkle.

I never appreciated my young body. I hated it. I picked it apart. I treated it disrespectfully. I didn't know what it was capable of. I didn't understand just how fabulous my body was. So, thank you for what I'm sure you meant as a compliment. I'm deeper than that though. I'm more, so much more that how I look after having three babies.

2. You look busy.

No shit. Are you kidding me right now though? I've got one kid kicking and screaming under my arm because you sauntered up behind me with a frozen yogurt treat. One of my children is trying to open a loaf of bread with his teeth and the oldest, most mature child, has strategically placed himself beneath the cart in front of the wheels to keep me from leaving the store because they are sampling red #40 laced gummy bears. Yeah, you could say I'm a bit busy. Or, you could join the party and ask me if there's anything you can do to help. I assure you, I'll only be awkward about it for the millisecond it takes me not to choke on my tongue from your extreme bravery and kindness.

3. You've got your hands full.

The cousin of 'you look busy' is generally spoken when a slap of obvious would be more appropriate. Again, if my upper lip is sweating and I'm trying to hold my shit together and not publicly embarrass myself by lying down in defeat, just lend a hand. Please, it would really make me feel less like you're an asshole and more like we're all in this together and the world is really watching my family grow and willing to help instead of just nosh on popcorn and laugh at my folly. Step out of the peanut gallery and into life on this one, please.

4. You're done now right?!

Done with what? Having sex? Tracking my ovulation cycle for perfectly planned conception? Seducing my husband with my hot post baby body? What the heck are you saying? Am I done being intoxicated by the scent of a freshly born scalp? Do I want to give up the stage of being a woman that has me feel beautiful and needed? Do I care what you think?

Listen guy/gal, I may be done having babies and I may want 10 more, either way, it's none of your beeswax and I intend to do what I want when I want until the law says I must answer to the random guy at the gas station. I love having babies. I love raising my beastie feral children and I haven't yet decided what is best for our family. Would you like a call when I do?

5. Oh, how perfect, two boys and a girl.

Right, it is perfect. So perfect for our family. We are blessed with two amazing boys and one extraordinary girl. They are perfect. It would also be perfect with two girls and a boy or a boy and a girl or one precious gift.

You see, I lost two babies and struggled to get pregnant with my oldest son. He was the best thing that ever happened to me. He showed me that nothing is ever impossible. Nothing. He showed me what perfect was. We had our second son so easily and then our daughter that I forgot how much strength it can take to bring people into the world. I then had two losses and realized that any combination of healthy children would be perfect. I have now lost more babies than I've birthed. Yes, my three children are perfect. Thank you.

So often we say things and give no thought to what it may mean for the recipient. I live in a world where I believe that we are responsible for what we hear and not what is said. We can make anything mean anything. I know that the people that say these things are just trying to tell me that they see me, they know my struggle or even that I'm doing a great job. I don't know their intention.

Usually I don't make it mean anything but some days when I've heard the same thing over and over and have had no real authentic interaction with someone in a while, I snap and choose to think the above responses.

That's ok too.

It is nice though when someone just shows me that I exist in their world too. When they offer to unload my grocery cart while I calm a fussy kid. When they smile and give a thumbs up when all of my babies are using great manners. Or, when they give a look of 'I've been there, it will pass' when they see I'm having a rough time.

I think the thing that triggers my knee jerk fist shaking is that the comments above don't feel human or genuine. It feels like 'how are you' and then walking away before an answer is given.

Stop. Think. Connect. Even if a person appears to have their act together they may feel like things are falling apart. A simple act of kindness can mean so much more than one thoughtless grouping of words.

PARENTING FAILS

I fail all the time. Especially if I compare myself to the ever increasing intricate measurements of parenthood as portrayed by the online realm. I'm an epic failure. As with most things, I think it shining a bit of light on them can help bring clarity and stop having everything be so damn significant.

So, here goes, some of my many failures, shared for your enjoyment.

1. I have photos up on my walls of my oldest child from birth to about 15 months old. Then, something happened... If someone didn't know us and toured our home, they'd be confused. There are toys and clothing for two genders from infant to preschooler but, no photographic evidence. I attempted to remedy this by putting a couple pictures of our two younger kids in some cheap frames on a dresser by the entry but it gets piled with stuff. So, if you ask my walls, I have one

child, suspended in time at around 15 months old. He's currently about to turn 5.

2. The edges of the insets of my kitchen cabinets are horrid. I'm talking disgusting crusty lacquered on mess of whatever build up can happen in the room of food. I once sat on a stool, 8 months pregnant, and used some Pinterest tip to scrub the shit out of those creases with a toothbrush. Once. Now, I give a cursory wipe and pretend I don't see the stuff I know would require more than a fingernail to scrape off.

3. Dust. Do I really need to explain this? I don't dust much. We live in a log home and dirt pretty much sifts through the walls and just lurks. Wiping it is futile as it only shows a streak of clean on a well covered canvas of dust artwork. I dust my walls with a broom when I sweep, if I remember, and about once a year I get that ridiculous brush tool out and vacuum the logs. Other than that, I baby wipe some surfaces and put away things that collect dust. I don't need daily reminders of those kinds of failures.

4. Baseboards. One of my pet peeves is dirty baseboards. It's like, for the love of all things holy, if you're going to clean the floor, wipe the damn trim too! But, I am completely humbled every time I sit on the toilet and notice, just out of reach, the thickening grime on the trim. Or, when I'm going up the stairs and I'm on a mission and realize that the banister boards are filthy...and I just keep moving to my destination. It's a choose your battles situation. I have over 3,000 sq ft to keep livable. I'm not a math person but that's a hell of a lot of trim to go with all that flooring. Ain't nobody got time for that.

5. Walls. It would appear that we have a finger painting circus living in our home. My mother-in-law calls it ring-around-the-house. I call it embarrassing. I honestly don't notice it until I stand proud, with hands on hips, admiring my clean floor and dusted table and then, notice, wait, is that a spaghetti noodle just dried up and clinging to the wall?!

The truth is, I've never been a neat freak. I've never been a domestic goddess. Perhaps there was a time when all the rooms in the house were tidy and our home was quaintly decorated but... I have the best intentions but I live in my head a lot. I make lists, like promises I'll never keep and I spend a lot of time imagining the day I'll have a housekeeper. I have never been the Suzy Homemaker cleaner but I did once have a clean home. Kinda.

Now, in my life, clean is a relative term I use to explain that there are no pests dwelling in the main living areas...except for the ones that climbed out of my uterus and mess up my never sparkling sanctuary.

Whatevs. We live here. I know our bathrooms always smells like pee. I know that our bedroom looks like a homeless camp. I know that our yard looks like a yard sale without a sign. Believe me, I know.

It is what it is.

I'm not going to clean it daily or be the mom with that perfect cleaning schedule. I'm just not. I won't beat myself up over it either. I never was that person, nor do I aspire to be. Your bed gets changed when you pee in it or when muddy foot prints or crumbs prevent you from a good night's sleep. It's just how it is.

I pick my battles.

PARENTING AS A HUMAN A.K.A WINNING

I got a lot of positive feedback on my piece that admitted my parenting fails. I had so many moms and friends tell me that it really made them feel like they were normal and that they weren't alone. I got to pondering that. If we feel so drawn together by shared supposed failure, can we be equally comforted by sharing our wins. I'm not talking about posting on social media, only photos taken at the best angle or glossing over reality by only sharing the highlight reel. I'm proposing we own our awesomeness in a way that creates power within us and shines through authentically for those around us.

1. I do laundry every day. Every. Day. I may not get it washed, dried and put away but I make the effort to at least wash and dry a load or put away some of it daily. It has helped calm and tame laundry mountain. A hill of laundry happened after vacation but I am chipping away at it and folding and hanging clothes late after the kids go to bed

and here and there. I did it once, I saw the floor and the counter at the same time. I'll do it again. I'm no longer the mom that complains about laundry. Now, dishes...that's another story.

2. I let go of being a label fearing girlie girl. I chopped off my silken locks and traded in my hooker wedges for flip flops and I'm owning it. I'm not a full on yoga pants mom but I'm comfortable where I am. I have my own style and I buy clothes that I like, that I'll wear and that I can afford. I shop my clothes at thrift stores, Costco and Walmart. I thankfully accept hand-me-downs from my younger sisters. I think Target is expensive and if I need a fancy dress I borrow it or buy it at Ross. I'm totally comfortable in my Justin Gypsies and Lucky jeans from 2004 with a $2 T Shirt. Giving up the importance of labels and clothing and accessories has given me the power to express myself and be comfortable with clothing. Seriously, it's just clothing. It covers your body and protects you from the weather. Why make it hard?

3. I'm totally zen with living in a sticky crumb pit. I remember, with much chagrin, while I was pregnant with my first born and on bed rest, I snapped at my Grammy about the way she had cleaned my house. Yes, you read that right. I freaked out, called my mom, mother-in-law and sisters. I went on and on about how she purposely wasn't doing anything right. She was purposely irritating me. She didn't wipe the baseboards or scrub the corners with a toothbrush. She left CLR in a toilet and etched the porcelain. She didn't put the dishes away right. She didn't use the right cleaner for the floor. It actually pains me to admit that I was that petty. Granted, I was hormonal, scared and no longer in control of my own home but my actions were horrible.

I can't even imagine feeling that way now. Being that ungrateful. Not even a little. When my sisters visit they always start cleaning the kitchen. It's the grubbiest room in the house and they do it without saying anything. They work around me and tell me to move over. They load the dishwasher wrong and put things away in weird places. They break things and eat my favorite foods. And, you know what, I love it. I absolutely love that they feel comfortable in my home and that they want to help me and know that I really do appreciate it no matter how they do it. Letting go gave me appreciation and adoration for the helpers in my life.

4. My kids have awesome manners and incredible empathy (is that two wins). They say please and thank you. They introduce themselves to strangers and say, 'My name is...nice ta meetcha.' They shake hands. They say 'may I.'

When someone is having emotions they notice and they ask the person if they are ok. They care about others and how their actions influence them. They give hugs freely and without prompting. What's better than that?

5. I cook from scratch and I'm damn good at it. I make homemade salad dressings and sauces and don't use packets. I make scratch soups and stews and I bake bread. I can whip up a batch of totally healthful cookies with whatever I have on hand and they're always awesome. I love to cook and feed my family and friends nutritious delicious amazing food and it warms my heart when they fill their bellies at my table.

6. I stay home to be a mom and to make our house worth coming home to. I don't complain about it because I enjoy it. It's my purpose and I have a lot of freedom. Yes, I'm limited in a lot of liberties but it's all relative. It's my life and I'm rocking it.

7. (Written a few months ago, see #8 below) I lost a shit load of weight and have kept it off for closing in on a year. Well, maybe not an exact shit load, more like 70ish pounds. I'm freaking proud of that accomplishment. I have been overweight since around 2008; I have had body issues since puberty and I'm finally totally over it. Sure, I gain and lose the same 5 pounds every few months but it's a choice and

I'm aware of it and not controlled by it. I went from a size 14 after the birth of my last baby (happily down from a 16 after my first two babies) to now a comfortable size 4. I am healthy and a great example to my family, friends and children. I love helping others and knowing what it's like to struggle helps me be compassionate to others journey.

8. I gained weight. I'm owning it. I got pregnant and didn't know it and struggled with what I thought was my sugar addiction rearing its head again. I had no idea I was pregnant until I was around 9 weeks. I had been fighting my normal pregnancy urge to eat toast and bread and avoid other foods with strong odors and textures the first few weeks and instead made it so much worse by making myself wrong. Then, guilt and shame meant I'd hide and eat and hate it and do it all again. Then, I miscarried. I ate my feelings and just stopped caring. Before I pulled my head out of that whole story I had gained 10 lbs. Damn it.

The choice was mine. I recommitted to fueling my body and my mind and let go of making myself wrong. My food feelings disappeared and before I could fully wrap my mind around losing weight again, I discovered I was once again pregnant. I'm owning it. So, I ate bread and cookies and chocolate and sloppy joes. Whatever. I also ate pizza. So, I was sad. So, I felt shame. So. Just, so. I am now feeding my body and my baby and although I have nothing to wear between my largest size and smallest size, I'm ok just being. I'm proud of myself for not wallowing. I'm happy to be healthy and I know that the extra weight will be gone when the time comes.

When I wrote this and left it in 'drafts' I had been spending a bit too much of my time reading mommy blogs and ScaryMommy blog shares and I am just so done with shaming and everyone trying to make everyone wrong or trying not to be too proud of their own accomplishments. Some of the then accomplishments have changed, even a few months later. I've added a few and taken a few out. This just shows how important is it to share victories now. Right now, when they are fresh.

I suck at a lot of things but I'm a freaking rockstar at more stuff. I know there are moms that hold in their little happy treasures for fear of seeming boastful or that they may be seen as condescending. Those little treasures, the light of the win, the feeling of triumph when we conquer a personal foe or climb a figurative mountain, why the hell not share that?! I'll clap for you like a sloppy joyous seal. I'll sing your name. I want to surround myself with people that feel comfortable being everything that makes them Them. And, that involves being awesome.

PART **6**

COMPLETELY
INCOMPLETE

"In choosing my
turbulence I
released myself
from the panic."

COMPLETELY INCOMPLETE

I have spent a lifetime fighting turbulence. I've gulped and gasped and lived inside of panic and fear. I've plunged to the murky depths of my reality and sat in the piercing silence on the smooth pebbles of the bottom of this body of water that churns in me. My fear has caused the fight. My desperation has been my plight. The rolling disaster of it all crashed and battered my stringent soul. I hid. I lurked. I kept something of myself from the light, the sun, life.

I nearly drowned so many times. I'd look up through the wavy glass surface and know my lungs would burst before I could break through that crystal barrier. I have felt the weight of it all pulling me down, dragging me, stones of indecision, self-righteousness and pretension tethered to arms and legs that succumbed to the tug of darkness. The fear and peace of taking one sweet liquid breath and knowing it would all end.

The fight I made, the frantic feet kicking to stay above the surface, the smiles I forced were an illusion. I was scared. I was terrified. I lived in a state of constant distortion. I couldn't be seen. I couldn't just be.

My fear...I'd be found out. Swimming in the sparkling ripples of the surface is acceptable. How could I be accepted if my constant struggle to stay afloat was discovered?

Ahh, sweet and utter abandon. Letting go. Giving up. Letting the water guide and pull me. It is pure oneness. I discovered that the water is just water. The struggle is momentary. The plunge and fight for air, glorious. I relish the introspection and loft of thought that I get when I am faced with the depths of this abyss of life. I yearn for it. When I tread water in the safety of the shallows I wither and feel my lungs grow weak from lack of use. I die a little with each safe and expected breath.

When I realized everyone is focused on their own swim, their own deep end, I had to come to the stark understanding that no one really cares about my struggle. I was struggling because I thought they cared. I'm different. I'm odd. That, for some reason, really mattered to me. I assumed it mattered to everyone else. I'm not really that different.

My truth is that, that's ok. I am me. I am all that I am and all that I am is someone that occasionally makes a dive to the bottom, gets dragged to the rapids or loses herself in an eddy. I'm ok with that now and because of that choice, the choice to let go of the fight, I no longer need to.

I know my mind has buoyancy. I know my soul can't be drowned. I know this because I have sat on that dark stony bottom and just let it all go. I accepted the depths and invited them in. They embraced and comforted me in a way that no person can. In choosing my turbulence I released myself from the panic.

The waves and tides come and go. I bob and move with the currents and flow. My heart is light and my mind is clear. Letting go, choosing me, living now...that's all it took to enjoy the swim.

SELF-EXPRESSED

To be fully self-expressed is to let go of the possibility that you may land a certain way for others. It is to be and say and do whatever the hell you want and allow other people the space to do so as well. To be, truly be, in any moment, is to let go of the need to not offend or to impress or to do anything 'in order to' for another person. It is only then that people realize that it doesn't fucking matter what anyone thinks of you or your mouth or what comes out of it. It's a moment of sweet and utter beauty.

UNFULFILLED COMMITMENTS

It occurred to me this evening that most, if not all, of the upset in my life revolves around not fulfilling on commitments I've made. Though I've understood this at great length and in theory and practice I've seen the power of this one discovery work incredible transformation in my life, I have never taken it apart in incremental doses. This evening, while discussing with a fellow Landmark seminar attendee, a certain upset he was experiencing, it was as if all the cards lined up for me. I stood in front of this man, being fully present to his concern and upset and yet completely aware of his speaking into my life.

The upset was irrelevant to the outcome of the conversation. What I got, completely and wholly, was a communication I had no idea I had been looking for.

I got that if a commitment, strongly held and intended, is something that is based in a result or outside my own actual control, I am setting myself up for complete and constant upset. If my commitment is based out of results then I have absolutely no power over it and all I'm left with is a reaction.

This breakthrough is completely relevant to this book and this experience because I've spent entirely too much time making myself wrong for not writing a book, not completing a book not being all the things I've been so committed to.

The missing piece to this is that I've been so tied up in the results driven commitments that I missed the point of being fully self-expressed.

Full self-expression for me means enjoying the process and giving myself freely and fully to a project until I just don't. And then, it means that I am free to be with the incompletion or the completion but it has nothing to do with my commitment.

I've made myself a failure. I've shamed and blamed and hung my head. I've made grandiose sweeping statements when in the biggest scheme of things, I just want to write beautiful and touching words, thought provoking moving pieces that may or may not flow or make sense in the context of what's currently expected by the publishing world, but fuckit, I am doing what I'm doing and I'm doing it the way I do. While complete in its incompleteness and scatter. The common tie is the ontology of living my life and experiencing myself as a growing and yet perfect being.

Even if I only experience that for a few seconds between self imposed upsets, struggles and imagined conflict. It's real. I'm real and I'm completely not making myself wrong for putting these words out into the world, just the way they are.

I heard one of my children make a declaration about themselves the other day and it occurred to me that he was creating himself, right there, in that moment. His declaration was shaping his day and possibly the trajectory of his life. I've since spent time being present to their 'I am' statements.

I am brave.

I am smart.

I am scared.

I spare them the conversation of 'being' and just observe and listen. The declarations shape the moments that follow. They act bravely, intelligently or fearfully. They act on those declarations.

The thing is, they aren't actually any of those things. That are just humans, pliable and extraordinary humans. Vessels of infinite possibility, ready for a command for action.

Being brave, being smart, being scared, they're all commands to the self. Commands to be in those spaces. Commands to take on a way of being that serves them. Some day we'll have these conversations. Someday. What are your declarations about yourself?
What do you say about yourself to others and to yourself?
How many times do you make declarations that don't align with your commitments and goals?

Words have so much power.
I am powerful.
I am beautiful.
I am infinite.
Try it on -- see if you smile.

IS IT A LIFE OR A LIFESTYLE

This morning as I was standing in my undies in the driveway digging clean underwear out of a large plastic tote, still strapped to a trailer from camping, I had a thought.

'What an odd lifestyle we have.'

And then, a rushing epiphany followed. Is it a lifestyle? Have we built a lifestyle? A context to live inside of. Have we built a shelter for our oddity in which we base decisions and make choices conducive to the growth of that world we've built? Or, are we just building and living our life?

I was thinking about that. I know people that live inside of a lifestyle. They pride themselves on their crunchiness or their earth friendliness or their upper echelon living. Their vehicle, clothing, home, career, it all lines up with this conceptual idea of an idealistic lifestyle. It all fits. I'm not saying this is bad. I'm just thinking out loud. I'm wondering if this perpetual cookie cutter shape we push ourselves into is the way to go.

I stood there enjoying the wind on my legs. I'm not a nudist. I just don't like pants. I looked at the windblown trees and marveled at their strength. I'm not an environmentalist but I have deep convictions about the earth and how we should treat it. I stood there really at odds with a life over a lifestyle and I couldn't force my lumps and bumps into any certain context.

I love the earth but I drive an oversized SUV and support logging and have almost 4 kids. My carbon footprint doesn't define me. I still feel how I feel about salmon and dams and the Amazon rainforest. I'm conflicted in my views so they just don't fit. Log all the trees...except those ones, don't cut those. Save all the salmon, but I'll eat it, I'll catch it and toss it on the grill. Please don't add to the mess of garbage in the floating island in the Pacific...but grab a case of bottled water at Costco before we head camping, because it's convenient.

Who am I?

Who are we?

I am whoever I say I am. I am me.

I can want to save the earth and still build a log cabin. I can create a life without the context of lifestyle. I don't have to be a 'crunchy' mom or a conservative or embarrassed that I'm an advocate of equality while I make my husband a sandwich, get him a beer and rub his back.

There doesn't have to be conflict in the lives we live. Our lives can be ideal without fitting an ideology of a lifestyle. I think the conflict arises when we try and stuff our lives into lifestyles and live out of a context that doesn't bring us joy. When we pass up opportunities like having more children, buying a bigger or smaller home or eating meat because it doesn't align with this non existent thing we lug around with us. It doesn't have to be perfect. It already is.

The being of our lives, the living it, the pure chaos of happenings and moving through the moments, that is the perfection. That is life. That is living.

Lifestyle and living are not the same. Not at all. When lifestyle becomes life, when it becomes us, our belonging, our freedom, our oppression, it is then that we no longer truly live.

I say, shake it off. Nothing means anything unless you say it does. This life, your life it is all in your word. The actions you take on those words. You get to say if you want to buy cage free eggs, and eat only organic produce and then have a milkshake at a fast food place. It doesn't define you. It just is what it is. It's living. No lifestyle can do it for you.

THE RIVER

There is in me a rushing river.

It flows and caps and spills over its banks.

It dries and trickles and meanders the smooth stones and sand.

The waters are warm and calm and frigid and crashing.

There are eddies that spin, with debris and filth, hiding vibrant growing life and scaled treading trophies.

There are forks that carve paths through ancient rotting ridges of formidable spires, that jut out with sharp edges, worn smooth, at the waterline, by time and temperament.

The depths of the river know no bounds and the secrets that lurk there are dark and leering.

The sun sparkles across ripples of joyous smooth, clear water, moving, ever moving toward a future unknown.

The shallows team with bright flitting life, darting, swimming, smooth as the cascade of colored stones they hide behind.

Rushing, ever rushing, swirling and churning; taking in fresh movement from glacial streams and cleansing rains.

The voice of the rushing waters roars in my ears.

The haunting moan tugs at my very being. And so, I must, I just must listen and obey.

The mist above capping rapids clears my mind as the groan of longing pierces my heart.

I must, I must...write.

SHE

She was chaos.
Twisting, churning, passion.
Her soul pressed against
The frame, neglected
Painted pretty.

Aching solitude
Spread out to infinitum
Edges dark and smooth
From wear.

Years of resistant pressing,
Fighting self imposed tethers,
Against the dreams
She denied.

She was conflict.
The daily struggle
Of pretending she
Was ok.

Being who she had become,
Was worse than admitting
She should
Jump ship and swim blindly for
Her dream.

The pull and turn of it
Twisted her so tight
She nearly
Broke with each insight
That she alone
Deprived her soul
Of the sustenance
That would sustain her
Aching heart.

She was contribution.
The sparkle and fade of
The steady and constant
Inner struggle and wane

Burst forth in her words
Landing barbed and sweet
The tempest tossed
The pain forgot

True passion propelled
The intent of connecting
So much stronger

Than the tug of defeat

She gave and launched
Herself off the ledge
Knowing the net was never
Going to be what caught her.

Her words,
Shared freely,
A soul strewn about.
Not once considering
The impact of tumbling pebbles
From climbing above
The noise.

WE SEE WHAT WE LOOK FOR

When you think about your life journey, do you ever wonder why it often takes so long to fully experience the newest version of you? Do you ever wonder why you don't feel transformed or changed and then one day, it all hits you at once?

We often get caught in the trap of looking at the negative or unwanted things in our life. We look for all the things we wish to change. We look for the things we don't like about ourselves and we look for our failures. We pull pieces for conversations and bits of our day to support this idea we create that the world is a certain way.

We end up seeing only what we are looking for.

If you doubt this, buy a new white car and then try not to be surprised by all the white cars that are now on the road with you.

The science behind it is vastly important to our personal development but the long and short of it is that you can pivot a simple behavior and completely transform your life.

Spend the next week looking in the mirror for all the proof that you are amazing. Look at your life for all the proof that your goals are moving into completion. Look at your family as if they are interacting with you as whole and complete.

See what comes of looking for what you want to see. Look, even if it's never been there before, look.

Look for your dreams.

Look for your passions in others.

Look for the worth and beauty of your being.

Look for it and you will see it.

Just look.

THE BETTERROOTS

Every year I wait patiently for the Lewisia rediviva (Bitterroot) to bloom.

This year it's been a long wait. Each time I go on an adventure around the property I get down and examine the plump succulent leaves. Tiny bursts of green against the rocks they sprout from. Like juicy fingers clambering for the spring sun.

I've been watching and waiting and searching through the photos of the past to gage when I could expect the vibrant blooms.

The wild stonecrop fared well over winter and all the leaves are full and green. Some of the usually small and struggling plants have taken on miniature shrub status. But still, no Bitterroots.

I was beginning to think I may have missed them. Perhaps I got the timing mixed up and maybe I had my information all wrong.

Many flowering plants die back after their showy blooms open up. All the energy required to put on such a visual display of power and life, it's too much to sustain. So the plant goes dormant or often dies completely. At least it's this way with succulents.

I feel like I need to be there, acknowledge their strength and will, honor their life, sit with and see their beauty. Missing a bloom feels a bit like missing a visit with a close friend. The ones that die off...well, you can ask my husband, I've cried a few times when I've missed their climax.

Ellie came in today yelling and yelling, amidst the chaos and bustle of coming home from picking up her brother, and I bristled. I've been running all directions lately and my well-being is a bit parched. I felt frustration rise, the noise and busy of it. I almost snapped.

Then I looked, I looked up from my phone timer, set for frozen chicken nuggets, and saw her face.

She beamed. The brilliance of pride danced in her sapphire eyes. Her tiny hands held two bouquets. One yellow and one a glorious magenta pink.

Lewisia rediviva.

I didn't miss it. My beautiful daughter was watching too and even as I imagined she wouldn't remember from last year, she watched.

"Mommy! The Better Roots are bloomed! They're everywhere! I brought you some and they're so perfect. Look!"

Ah, yes, the better roots. My sign of a beautiful summer opening up for us. The flower that can withstand an entire year without water and burst forth in a show of triumph. The flower that sacrifices its leaves to open its face to the sun.

Native Americans used to time their migration with the bloom of the Bitterroot. It's roots were so valuable you could trade a bag full for a live healthy horse.

The Bitterroots are blooming. I stuffed her bouquets in her special mug and then went out to visit them. They don't last long and because their leaves die when they bloom, by next week, there will be no sign that they even existed. Just dried up crepey vestiges of their beauty, blown by the thoughtless wind.

The stone crop appeared happy to be standing so tall and full among its long lost friends. The rocks even appeared proud, with their tiny pink crowns and showy sprouts.

My dried and cracking self plumped right up. It's not about the flowers, the waiting, the hope.

It's about the tiny pieces that pull together to create the loops that make it worth being present. The micro moments that remind me that I can choose not to be parched.

I can choose to look up and see the smiling faces or the sad crying faces. I can choose to let go of the loneliness fed by looking into a device. I can choose to bloom without water and push past the need for leaves to hold my worth. I can choose. It doesn't matter when, it always works out.

The Better Roots are bloomed.

My heart, its full.

LOVE IS A SPACE

Consider for a moment all the suffering that has been experienced through thousands of years of humans loving and being unloved. The gut-knot-face-flushed feeling of falling in love is a physiological response to a flood of chemicals in our bodies. That flutter of fulfillment contrasted with the sickening twist of falling away from that content adoration. All of that suffering for love.

Imagine a world outside the current context of love. Imagine a world where love wasn't a thing you felt but a way you interacted with life and the people in it. Imagine if love was something you brought to experience instead of gave to or got from someone. Imagine if you held that power and if you could remove the suffering of it all.

I invite you into that space. The space of complete responsibility and creation. The space where love isn't real.

The way humanity currently interacts and experiences the world is that love is to be achieved, felt, expressed, given and received. Consider that love is an idea that exists in agreement reality. It is only anywhere because we say it is. We enroll others in this reality and it's a beautifully tragic and lucrative thing.

It is believed that love is kind. Love is beautiful and love is arbitrary.

The impact of that context is that the unloved, unlovable and tossed aside have no power... it's on them. They suffer and they struggle. The pressure to deserve love, be better and bigger and more lovable is confronting. It filters our words and impedes our actions. It fosters a sense of reaching and finding and encourages us all to look outside ourselves. The reality of agreement shakes its head and looks away.

Imagine a world that we don't actually love, we create a space of love and invite others into that space and share it. In that version of reality, others exists as a space of love and share that space as well. There is no worth metric or giving and receiving. In this context love is an open space created by us to invite others into or share with them. It is not dependent on anything but our creation and experience of it. Imagine love as what we construct and say instead of what we earn or give.

As a person constantly at odds with my own lovableness I take power from being with this reality. I remove myself from the space of being unlovable and create my experience of love as my experience of myself.

No one is inherently lovable if love is merely a shared idea of what is so. It's arbitrary and divisive. No one is lovable. Consider that to be lovable is a made up construct to feed a reality created for safety. Safety and judgement. I'm a space for love to be expressed and shared. That's it. The rest is an agreement in which worth and value are up for popular vote. It's bullshit.

But what if God is Love?!

Oh, that is sure to come up in the dismantling of a paradigm. Always, fear says what if...

For the argument to end all argument, consider that God can be love in each reality. Consider that God is a space for everything to be expressed and show up. God created a space, we say what's in the space.

Imagine a world that left it available for you to have power over love. Imagine commanding and holding space as an expression of love as yourself.

Imagine.

A NOTE ON FEAR

I like to make declarations. I like to make goals. I like to make to-do lists. I like to dream up huge plans to get to amazing scenarios and I'm also deeply paralyzed by fear. Well, I can't say that is fully true because if it was, this book wouldn't be here. Let's just say, I am becoming aware of just how much of a hold fear has had on my life and just how much I give up because of things that have never and likely will not happen. Fear of failure is a universal condition. It really doesn't have to be. Failure isn't a thing. It means nothing. Due to the fear that surrounds failure we have given it undue value. It's really nothing and in nothingness we are free to create.

IF THESE WERE YOUR LAST WORDS, WOULD YOU SAY THEM?

As I scroll through post after post, throwing my time into the swirling vortex that is the FB time suck, I wonder... If I (you, we, whatever) were to die unexpectedly tomorrow and all that was left of me and my existence were the words I'd written, the photos and videos I'd shared and the impressions I've made on people, would I feel happy, fulfilled and complete?

A friend recently had a friend die in an accident and I snooped over to the deceased persons FB page. Beautiful. Adventures, happiness, humanitarian civic projects... Forever the most important things to him are memorialized. I have several people in my fb friends list that are now gone. I sometimes go visit their walls to get a piece of them, get inside their last thoughts. I miss them. I want to reach out and touch their souls. I want to see a bathroom selfie before they went to a scary important meeting. I want to read about how pissed they were that their coffee pot broke but that they now know the glory of drive thru coffee shops. I want to see a picture of their feet while they relaxed on a boat or beach or their deck. I want to smell their neck in a hug just one last time and as close to that as I can get is scrolling their fb wall and photos and everything they found important enough to share with the world.

If this is me. If these words are, someday, all that is left of the battle, the struggles, the passion, the love and the joy in my heart, am I saying everything that I should? Am I sharing myself in a way that my left-behinders could catch the slightest whiff of the lavender oil I wear when I'm nervous. Would these words fill a void in the reader's heart where the touch of my hand once calmed them? Will my leavings warm their being when they just needed to remember the rhythm of my chaos?

CURRENT OF NOW

It's funny how time moves. As a child I remember thinking a day lasted a lifetime. It took forever to complete a boring day. Yet, summer vacation flitted by like a hummingbird. I remember parents saying it only goes by faster as you age. Now, from where I stand, time lapping at my legs and charging my skin with possibilities and splashing my heart with urgency, I see it differently. I can only imagine the idea of time speeding up as one ages has a lot to do with watching the passage of time as it relates back to children.

As an adult I feel the flow of it as a voracious rushing current. Or as the rhythmic ebb and flow of waves meeting and leaving a beach, pulling the sand from beneath my feet as it recedes, leaving me in the same place but at a new perspective. The pulse of it is constant, a drumming in my soul, a constant metronome of awareness that it is moving with or without me.

As an observer of my own children I feel it as a ripping roaring coursing torrent. The days splash and gurgle, churning into foamy weeks and spiraling months. The years are engulfed by the breaks of the swell and the rising mist distorts and clouds. The drums wild beating grips my being and yanks it into a dance of fury.

Dance.

Dance to the beat of this moment. It is not a pattern nor is it a pulse. It leaps high and quick and dives low and steady. The shrill pitch and low hum are dizzying as the currents roll and rip and slosh and pool.

I can not for the life of me remember how I spent the days when it was only my first born and me. I physically strain to look back through the fog of his short life to see it.

Our routine. Our precious moments before he became a brother. Nothing. A dense fog of moments smashed so closely together I can't separate them into a linear memory. Emulsified and frothed into oblivion. Those tiny things I held so tight, ripped from my grasp by the rip tide of time. Yet, I can remember quite distinctly the day I broke my own arm at the age of 7. The musty scent of a wet and reluctant spring and the thrill of competing against my older cousin for the highest jump out of a swing. I never held that memory. I never tried to save it.

In just a year so little and so much can change. The word 'just' is the most ridiculous limit. Nothing is ever 'just' something. The gurgling twist of a tide is always there, pushing and pulling and pleading for acknowledgement. The beat beat beating of the heavy drum, demanding a march of progress. If anything is 'just' something it certainly isn't time.

Time is short, it is long, it is fleeting, it is the second that lasts lifetimes, it is the lifetime that flashes by. It is the steady beating of the patient heart and the rush of blood through the veins of the adventurer. It is now and that is all. It is the deepening of a voice. It is the subtle emergence of language where only days ago there was babble. Time is the scent of a newborn, now gone and replaced by the earthy smell of dirt and sunshine.

Time is this.
It is now.

This is dirt.

ABOUT THE AUTHOR

AMBER J. JENSEN

Amber is a lifelong writer and storyteller. She builds her word muscles day-jobbing as a content strategist and copywriter for a creative branding firm. Working the angles of different writing styles and what appeals to readers has given her a growth edge outside of general non-fiction or fiction writing. Coupled with years of continued education and ontological training, her prose makes its own path.

Shaping and sharing experiences through linguistic artistry is something Amber holds deep reverence for. Her desire to contribute to others through transparency and dripping authentic storytelling is what has her words stand out as otherworldly.

Amber makes her home on a piece of dirt in Eastern Washington, with her four wild children and adventurous husband. Wether she's writing from her phone near her family or down in the dirt building rivers and roads with her children, she does so while constantly observing the condition of being human.

She has created a life of dirt and adventure and contributes as much as she can to others that they may see the beauty in their own life dirt.

Look for Amber's future works of both non-fiction and fiction and learn more about her dirt road philosophy and upcoming title releases at www.amberjjensen.com.

Made in the USA
San Bernardino, CA
04 December 2017